JERRY SAXON

LIFE IS BUT A DREAM

LIFE IS BUT A DREAM

The colorful memoir of a physics teacher who deals with 15 years of bi-polar illness

JERRY SAXON, Ph.D.

authorHOUSE®

AuthorHouse™
1663 Liberty Drive
Bloomington, IN 47403
www.authorhouse.com
Phone: 1-800-839-8640

First published by AuthorHouse 09/09/2011

ISBN: 978-1-4567-9427-9 (sc)
ISBN: 978-1-4567-9426-2 (hc)
ISBN: 978-1-4567-9425-5 (ebk)

Library of Congress Control Number: 2011915090

Printed in the United States of America

SYNOPSIS

Beginning with a horrible nightmare of having been run over by a car when he was 8 years old, Dr. Saxon recovered to develop a strong interest in math and physical science. He won an award for excellence in math his senior year in high school. He obtained a B.S. degree with honors from M.I.T. and a Ph.D. from the U. of C. in physics. Just before graduating he developed a depressive illness that changed his life. He turned to Yoga, acting, dancing and assorted therapies before settling down at St. Xavier College. Depressions and hypo manic episodes haunted him for 15 years until he found long term help with a special psychiatrist. This book delves into the complex relations between the author, his family and friends. It describes many of Dr. Saxon's adventures in the classroom, his delightful trips to 25 of our national parks and his escapades with a variety of women.

DEDICATION

This book is dedicated to my father and mother
who gave me the love to experience life fully.

ACKNOWLEDGEMENTS

I would like to acknowledge the wonderful teaching of Mr. Bodwicz who instilled in me a love for science, Dr. A.V. Crewe, who guided me through the arduous work of completing my thesis and Dr. Henry Conroe who helped me through a normal life after 15 years of manic depressive episodes.

BIOGRAPHY

Jerry Saxon earned a B.S. degree in Physics at M.I.T. and a Ph.D. at the University of Chicago in Physics. He taught physics and astronomy at St. Xavier College and physics at Thornton Township High School in Harvey, Illinois. He also pursued his passion for photography by presenting over 150 travelogues of western national parks and over 15 foreign countries as well as creative work in Kirlian Photography and polarized light photomicroscopy. His favorite activity was dancing—thousands of dances from square dancing to folk dancing to ballroom dancing.

PREFACE

In April the breaking news on CNN was a report that a famous actress, Catherine Zeta-Jones, admitted herself into a mental institution for treatment of a bipolar disorder.

The video coverage was exotic. She was dressed in a flamboyant gown and her long hair flowed in the wind. She offered no explanation as to how she felt. She was released five days later. In two months she stole the show at the Tony Awards in New York.

A fair number of Americans probably know that well known actors, actresses, writers, painters and politicians have at times been diagnosed with manic depression—the former name for the disorder currently labeled Bipolar II Illness. Only the slightest information regarding her diagnosis and treatment of Bipolar Illness was made clear. Many books are available for more technical detail.

An extremely small number of Americans know that over 30 years ago a young science professor teaching at St. Xavier College in Chicago felt that he was having a "nervous breakdown" and drove himself to the mental ward of a hospital in the western suburbs of Chicago. No cameras, microphones or reporters were present. I was that science professor. It was the first time I was hospitalized in a mental institution but not the last time. The diagnosis was not made clear to me but two weeks later I was released labeled fit to return to my normal routine. A CAT scan of my brain showed normal patterns as explained by my doctor, except I had lost the ability to read beyond the second grade level. I felt like an 8 year old child. The fall semester was coming up in 6 weeks and I was scheduled to teach Physics, Astronomy and Physical Science. I was given no follow up instructions that I recall and was not mentally capable of inquiring about such instructions.

My girlfriend generously looked after my basic needs and I spent a lot of time with her. I had no family in Chicago but set out to investigate several alternative medicine approaches to solving my problem such as acupuncture and chiropractic. Eventually I described my situation to a friend from the college and he recommended a psychiatrist he thought would be helpful. The psychiatrist prescribed Nardil, a MOA Inhibitor. My head cleared and my mental ability fully recovered just a few days before I began teaching. For about fifteen years after this event I endured depressions and hypo manic episodes ranging from having no desire to live to feeling I was in the company of God himself.

I have attempted to explore the interaction of problems in living with the genetically induced disease of manic depression and tried to write in a style that is simple and easy to understand yet conveys significant information. Please do not think of this memoir as a recipe for curing Bipolar Illness but rather the personal account of an intelligent but flawed man who attempts to make the most out of his life. Some of the names in the book are actual names, but in other cases where I totally forgot the actual name or did not want to reveal the real name I made one up.

My hope is that my readers will become more familiar with a disease that can be devastating yet heighten the loftiness of the feelings that we as human beings can fathom. I have recorded some of the most personal aspects of my experiences. I hope you will find some entertainment along with knowledge in the following pages and read without judgment some of my more severe episodes.

CHAPTER 1
CHILDHOOD

Stroudsburg is a small town in Pennsylvania, south of the Pocono Mountains. I spent my childhood there in the late 1940's. We lived in a fairly large corner building on the second floor. My father was a doctor and had his office on the first floor. My sister was three years younger than I and I practically have no memories of her during this time. I attended grade school a few blocks away at the top of a gentle hill. There was a large playground in the back of the school where we enjoyed recess. We got report cards several times a year and rated either below average, average or above average in each subject. I must have been a pretty good student because most of my grades were above average. My lowest grade was below average in Music. I don't remember the names of any of my teachers but they were all women and treated me well. My 6th grade teacher was especially fond of me and spoke highly of me to my mother.

After school I played mostly with my best friend Dougie, short for Douglas. He lived only a block away and we built forts in an open field behind my home. Every afternoon at 5:30 a few of the kids in neighborhood met at Kristy's house. She was the first girl in my class living nearby who had a TV in her living room and we sat quietly on her couch and watched Howdy Doodie. Buffalo Bob may have been the leader of the group, but my favorite character was Princess Summer Fall Winterspring. What a great name and creative costume.

One afternoon while playing in the field I was crawling along the ground and noticed blood coming out of my lower leg. Frightened, I ran to my father's office. The blood was due to a cut I got while crawling over a broken bottle. My father wanted to sew up the wound, but I was scared and he settled for a bandage. Soon a scar formed, but the incident was minor compared to one that was to come shortly.

My grandparents lived in Scranton, an hour away from Stroudsburg, and we visited them for Jewish holidays. I remember Passover the best with the grown-ups sitting at the big table and the kids sitting at the small table down at the end. I vaguely remember my great grandmother who was revered although she hardly spoke. I had little interaction with my grandmother who also hardly spoke. Grandfather of course led the Seder entirely in Hebrew. The service seemed especially long and I was impatient for the meal to begin and very bored with the grace after the meal. I still have some of that impatience today.

Yiddish was spoken frequently which was frustrating because I could understand very little. During the summer the family spent time in several trailers in fields outside of a small village called Gouldsboro. There was a lake for swimming and a railroad track that ran through the area. I would enjoy watching the railroad cars go by and counting them as they did. Particularly impressive were the trains that had over 100 cars. Also enjoyable was picking huckleberries that grew nearby and my mother using them to bake pies. Once a week I went upstairs from the General Store where they showed cowboy movies. Gene Autry, Roy Rogers, Lone Ranger were the highlight of my week.

Back in Stroudsburg we got a TV. My favorite show was the Lone Ranger. I frequently played alone in my bedroom. I had a cap pistol and would stand near the window that looked out on an alley. I imagined the bad guys shooting up at me in the window, but I would kill them with my pistol.

Next door lived Barbara, a girl about my age. We would take a blanket out in the alley, pull the blanket over our heads and play "doctor". We would slowly take off all of our clothes and pay close attention to and examine our genital regions. I noticed that my penis would grow larger during our play, but of course I didn't understand why. There were no computers at this time so our games were imaginative and involved close contact and interaction with each other.

Another game that was fun was flipping baseball cards. Almost every boy in the neighborhood collected baseball cards. We stood about five or six feet away from a building wall and took turns flipping a card toward the wall. The boy whose card came closest to the wall would win both cards. The challenge was to get your card to lean up against the wall, called a "Leaner", which almost always would be a winner. On Thursday afternoons I would walk close to a mile to Hebrew school where we would learn stories from the Bible and Elementary reading in Hebrew. I have practically no memories of the teacher or actual classes but there is one day that I left home for Hebrew school that I will never forget. I was late and in a bit of a hurry but after crossing my street I remembered I forgot my watch and turned around and went back to cross the street to go to my house and get the watch.

The next thing I remembered I was laying in the street and my head hurt. A few people had gathered around and I could hear voices but could not see anything. Much later I found that a car had hit me and one of the front wheels of this large car had run over my midsection. My forehead had scraped the pavement as I fell and was the only place that was bleeding. There were no broken bones. I was taken to the local hospital, placed in an oxygen tent and put on the critical list. My stomach began to swell up but the doctor did not know exactly what was wrong with me. I was eight years old.

The details of what came next are very vague and came mostly from what my parents told me after I had recovered from this accident.

The scrape on my forehead healed quickly leaving no internal damage but a scar that lasted many years. The view inside the oxygen tent was bleak. I could not distinguish individuals and was very thirsty. "Water! Water! Please bring me water!" I remember shouting. Eventually a nurse brought me a few ice cubes to suck on.

My father temporarily turned his practice over to another doctor and spent most of his time by my side. The hospital doctors didn't know what to do so my father brought in a surgeon from New York. There were no MRI's in those days and the decision was made to make an incision down the middle of my stomach. There was internal bleeding and damage to the stomach and other nearby organs. A decision was made to punch a hole in my right side at the stomach level to continuously drain fluid through a tube into a bag. After a week I was taken off the critical list and transferred to a nice bright hospital bed with a clear view of the park outside. I stayed in one position for several weeks except for turning my behind so that a Penicillin shot could be injected into my backside twice a day. I resumed eating simple meals, got a lot of "Get Well" mail from friends and tried to keep up with my school work using my class books. After six weeks I began to learn to walk again holding onto the railing from the wall. Eventually I came home. It was weeks before I returned to school but had kept up with my lessons.

I remember being irritable and cranky, my father not being around for a while and my mother pressuring me to claim that I had looked both ways before entering the street when the car hit me. There were unsolved matters of insurance and how much money in benefits I would collect. I simply don't remember the intricate sequence of events that lead from entering the street to lying helpless under the car. My parents felt that two of the witnesses to the accident claimed it was my fault because I was a Jewish boy and the driver of the car was a good Christian. The Jewish population of Stroudsburg was very small. Gradually the conflict of the entire incident was forgotten. I collected $2,200 on my 21st birthday and the street where the incident occurred was made one way for the sake of safety.

My father was very upset by the whole affair and gradually made plans to move to New Haven, CT where we had a number of relatives and there were many more opportunities to lead a fuller life. My father bought a modest house with a nice back yard, a shed and a grape arbor. We were just one mile from Yale University dorms and the Downtown New Haven Green.

I finished grade school in the Roger Sherman School and remember many details of my life in sixth grade. Most prominent was my infatuation with Donna, the girl who sat in front of me. We met on the corner two blocks from the school and walked together talking about this and that. We continued talking during class. Our teacher seemed to love children and teaching and was especially fond of me giving my mother glowing reports about the "boy with those wonderful warm brown eyes". Around Valentine's Day I bought Donna, my girlfriend, a box of candy, Tootsie Rolls, and wrote her a long letter of my infatuation to go with it. I put the candy and letter in my top dresser drawer where my mother, in her nosey way, found the candy and note and came to me with words of how cute this all was.

I was terribly embarrassed by this incident and never gave Donna her Valentine's Day present, but I did develop a resolve to show her my affection. Walking home together one day I asked her to come up a flight of steps with me, leaned over and kissed her firmly on the cheek and then ran down the block. Later as I passed her house she invited me in for some chocolate brownies that she had made. I was thrilled.

When 6th grade ended we went to different junior high schools. I went to Troup Junior High. She went to Sheridan Junior High. For several years I fantasized meeting her again and all the things I would do for her. I would imagine seeing her in a crowd. She was my first love, my puppy love. I've never forgotten her.

After school my favorite TV show was "Time for Blinky". Each week they had a contest with a different theme. Around Thanksgiving the theme was to draw your best turkey. I won! The prize was a new Schwinn bicycle which my father helped me learn to ride. My picture with the bicycle was in the local paper. The bicycle was stolen two years later.

My father was a Boy Scout in Scranton and became the first Jewish Eagle Scout in the city. I joined the boy scouts but never rose above the rank of "Star Scout". During summers I went to Boy Scout Camp, which was a lot of fun. But I was different from the rest of the campers in that I brought along an Algebra book and worked out Algebra problems in my spare time. I had a natural interest in mathematics and science. The night sky fascinated me I learned the names and positions of most of the bright stars and constellations and with a small telescope found craters on the moon, rings of Saturn and the four moons of Jupiter. Along with a few friends, we went up on my roof and marveled at the Milky Way and assorted sights through my telescope. It was dark enough in our back yard to see thousands of stars. Victor, a boy in my class, who became my closest friend, together with his father's help built an eight inch reflecting telescope that could see the polar caps on Mars and many star clusters. The knowledge I learned about Astronomy at this time was sufficient to teach an Astronomy course in college.

I loved Math and read Math books like most kids read Comic books. After graduating junior high my parents treated me to my first big trip from New Haven. A month's adventure by bus to Taos, a bus out to Philmont Scout Ranch, New Mexico. The icon of the ranch was a huge outcropping of granite in the shape of a tooth that could be seen from miles around called the "Tooth of Time". On a hike through the ranch I left the group and wondered off by myself to get a closer look at the tooth. This tendency to break from a group became a lifelong pattern.

CHAPTER 2
HIGH SCHOOL

When confronted with Shakespeare and the meaning of poetry I was lost. I went to friends and my father for help but mostly to no avail. The problem of being confronted with lines of words that had no meaning to me was so frustrating at times I was on the verge of tears.

I worked as a waiter at Camp Laurelwood during the summer after my sophomore year. I got together with two other waiters during the afternoons and we began a routine of running. This became a positive addiction which lasted for many years. I also took up tennis and played Intramurals later in college. Tennis became a consistent sport for most of my life. I was 14 and overall I enjoyed the experience of being a waiter. The counselors were at least four years older and I found myself desperately adoring a gorgeous red head with a fantastic figure. I never had the nerve to actually talk to her but I can see her in my mind 50 years later. Feelings of yearning for girls was still new to me and although I was too shy to actually express interest in most of them I had frequent fantasies at night of what I would do with a nude girl.

The girl I took a special interest in was Karen who was my date for junior high graduation at the local amusement park. Although she was emotionally distant she was very bright and independent. I was attracted to her and found a common interest in tennis. We would play occasionally in the early evening and when I took her home I would suggest getting a bite to eat or taking a walk but she usually rejected my offers. I was very sensitive to rejection and would feel badly thinking that she didn't find me interesting or attractive enough to spend more time with me.

On my way walking to school I would meet Carla on the corner and we would walk together discussing class work or more advanced subjects in Science. Her father was a professor at Yale. She was very friendly but I had no sexual interest in her. During this time I learned to make a distinction between girls who were sexually appealing and those that I enjoyed conversing with.

But things were changing in my body. Frequently I would awake in the middle of night to find that I had "wet my bed". Not understanding this as a normal wet dream I would find a towel and try to dry the sheet. I was ashamed that my mother would find the wet spot and be angry with me. At some point in high school I found that rubbing my penis with my hand until I came (I didn't know what the word ejaculate meant) was not only a very pleasant experience but a strong urge. If I wet my fingers with saliva the experience was even more pleasurable. Another particularly satisfying experience was to leave a soft sock near my bed and when I had the urge simply place the sock over my erect penis and rub gently. This way I achieved the most pleasure with no embarrassment. I continued this habit into my college years. I read quite a bit during this time but one book I remembered most clearly was "Peyton Place". I found secluded places to read it and finished it quickly. I kept in under my bed and hoped my mother would never find it.

But most of my time was spent on school work and my interest in Science and Math. In addition to building and firing rockets, building and using telescopes, I built a FM tuner with the help of my father. I loved math books and was fascinated with the idea that some infinities are larger than others. I would spend hours working out Advanced Algebra problems and eventually taught myself Differential and Integral Calculus a year before we encountered these topics in Advanced Math class.

My uncle Harry, one of my father's younger brothers, was a big influence in my developing an interest in Math and Science. He gave me a slide rule for my thirteenth birthday and I would ask him to give me interesting math problems to work out. He lived in New Jersey and during Thanksgiving we drove to Lakewood to spend the holiday with him and his family. My grandfather would also come and made a large pot of soup. I read issues of Scientific American, a magazine that Harry subscribed to and we took walks around a nearby lake. It was a happy, festive relaxing time.

Our advanced math class teacher, Miss. Malone, was also our homeroom teacher. She was not well suited for teaching Advanced Math and several of the students in my class would occasionally show her how to solve a problem. She was a slight short woman who wore practically the same clothes every day. Thinking back to the Tip-Top Bread commercials, she was the essence of the Tip-Top lady. Her constant repetition of certain phrases would lead many of us to stifle laughter. "Quiet at two, people, quiet at two, people" is just one of the phrases we kept records of. Many years later when I was teaching Science I thought of Miss. Malone and how little respect we showed for her. I was aware of my own peculiarities and wondered how my students viewed me.

During the summer after my junior year I was accepted into the Pre College Science Center with a scholarship at the University of Bridgeport, CT. I chose Physics as my specialty. During the six week course I met interesting students who had similar interest as I did. We studied College Physics and worked on a physics project with a partner. I worked on a simple cloud chamber that showed tracks of radioactive particles. For recreation I played a lot of chess and bridge. We also had to prepare an hour lecture on a physics related topic. I chose the Universe as my topic because of my interest in Astronomy. After the lecture I realized my talk would have been more effective if I had narrowed down my topic.

My senior year in Hillhouse was exciting in a number of ways. It was 1960, an election year, and we were thrilled about Kennedy becoming President. In October, Kennedy came to speak on the New Haven Green before 50,000 cheering people. On the way to hearing him speak, my friends and I removed a bottle of wine from the ledge of a Yale dormitory and finished it off during the speech. Kennedy spoke as if he had already won the election. His audience was highly partisan and there was electricity in the air.

It was also the year of applying to college. There were no doubts in my mind, MIT was my first choice. I also applied to Yale but didn't really want to stay in New Haven. The dedication of so much of my early life to math and science clearly made MIT my first choice. My application was very rich in science activity. I had the president of a local power company and graduate of MIT write me a letter of recommendation. My SAT Advanced Math score was over 800. When I got my letter of acceptance in April I was totally thrilled. I was the only senior going to MIT from Hillhouse High.

As a senior I was elected President of the Chemistry Club. But my first love was Physics. The only physics teacher in Hillhouse, Mr. Hodge was very good. He taught the classes a lot like college classes are taught, assigning weekly problem sets. There was also a term paper required. My topic was the Uncertainty Principle, usually not taught until Quantum Mechanics is introduced in college. The idea behind the uncertainty principle was first realized by the great physicist, Werner Heisenberg, and claims that where very small particles like protons are concerned it is impossible to measure both the position of a proton and its velocity at the same time with 100% accuracy. Not for a lack of the needed technical tools but simply because that was the way the micro cosmos works.

I did not like my English teacher, Dr. Sheridan, who was very strict and gave us much work to do but I remember her most for her incessant stories about the times she had tea with famous authors and poets like Carl Sandberg. She did teach us how to make an outline and write book reviews which turned out to be very helpful.

I hardly dated much in high school but a few incidents remain with me. I was attracted to Susan and called her for a date. We talked quite a while but when I asked her to go out she said she was busy that day but asked if she could have a "rain check". I had no idea what a rain check meant and was too embarrassed to ask. The conversation became very awkward but eventually we made plans to see the Kingston Trio. It was the height of the era of folk music which was very appealing to me. Susan was very talkative and spent most of the time expressing her total dislike of Senator Kennedy and her fears about the country going to Hell if he should be elected President. I had little interest in politics but knew my parents were Democrats so I took a liking to Democrats also.

Of course the big event at the end of senior year was the senior Prom. I did not go to the junior prom and still had not learned to dance. My friend Jerry had a girlfriend, Phyllis, who volunteered to teach me the basics of dancing. I practiced quite a bit and did okay when it was time for the prom, but the real enjoyment of the event came later when a few friends met for a party after the dance in Danny's basement. Danny had kept the lights down low and lit a few candles. After some small talk each couple found a place to snuggle up and make out. This was the first time kissing passionately and feeling our bodies pressed firmly together. I found it very satisfying and yearned for more. About four o'clock in the morning we decided to drive up to the top of West Rock Park the northern boundary of New Haven and watch the sun rise over the city. It was a wonderful way to break ties with Hillhouse.

About a year or two before I graduated high school my father bought a small cottage on Lake Quonapogue, about 20 miles from New Haven. The cottage was quite rustic with running water a pot belly stove for heat and an outhouse close by. It had a wonderful lawn that led to a dock on the lake with a rowboat and a beautiful large Weeping Willow tree near the lake. A small stream ran along the cottage down into the lake, which made a lovely sound to which to fall asleep.

I spent considerable time during the summer at the lake either alone or with friends. But I frequently yearned to be back in New Haven where there were friends and things to do. My most memorable Sundays were spent on the lake during the winter when the ice on the lake was close to a foot deep. There was a strong wind blowing from the north. We started from the north end of the lake with our ice skates on and held our arms out. The wind carried us to the south end of the lake with a good speed.

But there was a wonderful large white duck that became very friendly in return for food scraps. In an effort to expand and upgrade the cottage my father designed a large add-on room and a driveway. The plans called for a large picture window looking out to the lake and a separate indoor bathroom. Several of our neighbors on the lake offered to help my father with this project. I was restless and wanted to go into New Haven or go swimming and boating on the lake. I offered little help on my father's project which I later regretted since it would have been a good learning experience and provided assistance in return for all my father had done for me. The room was finished in several months. It upgraded the status and value of the cottage and nearly doubled its total space.

In an attempt to improve my English skills I hired a tutor who was a Yale professor. He assigned books to read and then we discussed them. The author I remember most clearly was Faulkner. At the same time I dated a girl my sister recommended, Sally, who was several years younger than me. She was six inches shorter but had very large breasts for her age. I can't recall any interests we had in common or any conversations we had but I do remember the sessions we had making out vigorously.

The summer after high school went by quickly. I was very excited about leaving for Boston and packed all my needed supplies and belongings in a large trunk. I took the trunk by train to Boston and then by cab to the Sigma Alpha Mu fraternity house which I had been invited to join. I was in a pledge class of ten guys mostly from New York. The fraternity house was in Boston's Back Bay area. To get to classes we usually walked to the Mass. Avenue Bridge and hitched a ride across the bridge to the MIT campus. If we had extra time, walking across the bridge was good exercise.

I shared a room with Leon, as sophomore from Michigan who went out of his way to be helpful and answer all of my questions. He had a very friendly manner. The room was small and I had the lower bed of the two level bunk beds. Pledges were given the job of keeping the house clean.

CHAPTER 3
COLLEGE

My class schedule was a little different from average. I opted to take an Advanced Level Calculus course and an optional class–A seminar with about ten guys in special relativity. I was well prepared and got the highest grades in my pledge class at the end of the first semester: 4.8/5.0.

I got along well with my pledge brothers. We helped each other with homework and I played Intramural track, tennis and football. We had frequent parties on Saturday nights which consisted of dancing and drinking. I didn't care much for beer but was raised on drinking wine. Hard liquor was new to me. One week I got a lower grade on a chemistry quiz than I would have liked. I bought a fifth of Old Crow Bourbon and drank more than a half of it. At the next Saturday night fraternity party I remember losing control and falling halfway down a flight of steps. I don't remember what happened to my date, but I remember crawling into my bed feeling nauseous. I couldn't sleep and made it just in time to the bathroom to throw up. I still couldn't sleep and made it a second time to throw up in the toilet. It was the first and last time that I ever got drunk.

We had two special weekends at MIT, one in the fall and one in the spring. The highlight was always a big named popular entertainer on Saturday night with dancing and drinking. I usually brought vodka and fruit juice which would get my date drunk without her being especially aware. Our first guest entertainer was Ray Charles whose music I am still especially fond of. Spring semester we had Fats Domino singing. It's strange that I can somewhat remember the lines of his songs recorded in 1962 but I can't remember a single line of any popular song from 1990 to the present.

During Christmas recess my father let me borrow his car and I went to New York to take Karen out to dinner on New Year's Eve. It was very exciting for me. Karen was in school at Barnard College. We both had matured somewhat since high school.

My second semester at MIT was somewhat uneventful. There are several experiences as part of pledge week that stand out. One night all pledges were blind folded and told to remain sitting in the dark until they were notified otherwise. It became frustrating and annoying to remain in a high back chair where there were no sounds in complete darkness. My head would fall forward but it was impossible to sleep. Everyone remained in their chairs. Finally a few brothers came into the room and said "Very Good, Very Good. You can go to bed." The following night we were told we would be rewarded for faithfully following instructions. One pledge at a time was led into one of the fraternity rooms that had been decorated with red lights and candles. We were told by the brothers that a prostitute had been hired for our pleasure and she was waiting in a bed on the opposite side of the room.

When my turn came I waited near the door and surveyed the scene. There was a body under a blanket on the bed and a head with blonde hair was clearly visible. The body motioned for me to come forward but I was too embarrassed to make any moves. Soon one of the brothers came out of the closet and told me to forget about it and I left the room by the same door I came in. I heard that the brothers got a good laugh from the more aggressive pledges who tried to get into bed with the mock prostitute. Amongst all the pledges spirits were high in the fraternity house.

Bridge games would be found going on in the house after homework was complete on weekdays and as brothers came home on weekends after a date. I really enjoyed the game and played frequently.

When summer came I returned to New Haven and found that my father had gotten me a job working for Cott Bottling Company that provided soda drinks in the Connecticut area. I started out on an assembly line lifting crates of soda bottles onto a conveyor belt where the bottles were later filled with soda. It turned out constantly lifting crates of bottles was too strenuous for me and I was transferred to a job sitting and watching filled bottles go by in front of a light panel and pulling any bottles out that contained any foreign material like cigarette stubs. This job, eight hours a day, was very boring and again I requested a change in job position. This time I got lucky and was placed upstairs in what they called the "Lab". Where I assisted Larry Landon in making the flavored syrup that would eventually be mixed with carbonated water to make the quart bottles of soda.

A batch of syrup was made by combining a large amount of heavily sugared water with several pitchers of concentrated flavoring which I carried from a large walk in refrigerator, up a short flight of steps and dumped into a 250 gallon stainless steel tank where the syrup was made. Finally a job that was easy and not boring because I could chat with Larry Landon, read the newspapers or read books on Physics in my ample spare time. My father would pick me up at the end of the day and we usually went up to the cottage which was less than 30 minutes away.

On weekends I sometimes borrowed my father car, a 1961 Rambler Sedan with push button transmission and a front seat that folded down into a bed. I went out with Libby and we would go to a secluded spot near the Yale athletic fields, put the front seat down, stretch out on the bed and make out for several hours. Occasionally a patrol car would come quietly by and the patrol man would shine his light into the window indicating we needed to move. Since we were mostly undressed it was a little embarrassing but we went on to find another dark area or just went home.

When I wasn't spending time with Libby I would spend Saturday nights with my father. One of my father's greatest pleasures was going to a steam bath (the old time baths he recalled going to with his father back in the late 20's near Scranton, PA). He actually found such a steam bath located on a farm about 25 miles north on New Haven. It was run by a Polish farmer from the old country (Eastern Europe) known simply as Pete. Located in an old barn on two levels, the steam room itself was on the bottom level. A large number of good sized boulders were located outside the room. Access to the boulders was made through an iron door that could be opened or closed.

Early on Saturday mornings Pete would gather a large bundle of wooden logs which he placed under the boulders. At the right time he would light the logs and let them burn throughout the day into the night. The burning logs would heat the boulders quite hot. Inside the steam room a man would throw a bucket of water onto the boulders and a rush of steam would come pouring into the steam room. The room itself had a lower level bench which was relatively cool and an upper level bench where the men took turns lying down while Pete gave them a wash with a bunch of oak leaves tied together and put in a basket of soapy water. The temperature was quite high on the top bench and many of the men used a cool wet towel over their heads to remain comfortable.

After getting thoroughly washed the man would step down on the floor and another guy would pour a bucket of ice cold spring water over him from head to toe. He then had a choice, either an ice cold shower in the adjacent room or in the winter going outside into the snow and rubbing the snow over his body. As if that weren't enough sometime later the man would come back into the shower and lie on a wooden table while Pete gave him a rubdown with alcohol. Of course this would sting because you could get scratched by the pressure of the oak leave wash and the alcohol would cause a stinging sensation.

Finally you would go upstairs into a large room where you had several options. If tired you could take a nap in a dark section of the room. If you were hungry there were all kinds of breads, meats and cheeses that could be made into sandwiches and the men sat around telling stories from the old country or in another section of the room a TV was always playing and you could watch everything from westerns to "Your Hit Parade".

If I didn't have other plans it was my pleasure to join my father in a visit to the steam bath. We had lively conversation and my father insisted on giving me a full wash and alcohol rub. I never built up enough nerve to have a bucket of cold water thrown over me and took the cold shower instead. For the rest of my life I've gone to modern steam rooms, saunas and whirl pools but none compared to the experience of Pete's steam bath. One night especially stands out when a man came to the bath who was of normal height but had a penis that hung practically to the floor (at least as I remembered it). He would grab it in the middle and swing it around making a surreal sight.

After my alcohol rub I'd get out my Physics books and work on problem sets. Occasionally the men would break out into songs from the old country. Although I offered to give my father a wash he would always refuse. I considered this experience my father and I shared as about as intimate as any we had.

As the summer came to a close I prepared for sophomore year at MIT. Prior to leaving I spent a week or so relaxing at our cottage. The added room was complete and the extra space was most welcoming. I noticed my father seemed tired quiet often possibly from the hard work of putting in the extra room and making a driveway up to the cottage. I picture him lying on a lounge chair often sleeping but didn't give it a second thought. During the summer I studied third semester calculus and took an Advanced Placement exam in the subject, got a B and was able to take fourth semester Calculus during the fall semester.

When I returned to MIT in the fall I decided to take sophomore courses that could be used for Pre Med such as Biology. Because the fraternity house had room for only 25 members, fifteen members had to share an apartment in the area. I chose to share a three room apartment with two guys in my pledge class, George Block and John Ross. The apartment was about three blocks from the fraternity house where we had all our meals and social life. My room was fairly small but big enough for a bed and a desk. The apartment was in a somewhat seedy neighborhood. One night a bat flew into my room and it was an ordeal getting it out.

One day in October, George approached me and asked if I would like to get laid. He said he had been dating this girl who fucked like a bunny and he was through with her "Would you like her number?" he asked. I said "Yes, what the Hell" and I called her asking if she would like to go to the movies. Her name was Sally. She was not very attractive but seemed intelligent and enjoyed conversation. She suggested we see "Lawrence of Arabia". My taste in movies at this time was mostly for adventure, thriller type films, but I wanted to please her even though I knew nothing about "Lawrence of Arabia".

When we got out of the movie she couldn't stop talking about what a great film it was and saw the director as being superb. It seemed like a lot of sand and Arabs to me but I listened carefully to what she had to say. It wasn't until about a year later after seeing the movie called "Blow up" that I began to gain some sophistication in understanding great movies. Anyway, we went back to my apartment and sat in the living room for a while. I suggested we go into my bedroom where it might be warmer. Since it was still chilly I suggested we get under the blanket. After removing our clothes I felt very awkward but after snuggling together for a while we somehow managed to make love with her being very cooperative.

After I took her home I was very excited that I had finally gotten laid. I went back to the fraternity house, found a few guys talking and playing cards and told them of my first sexual experience. We compared notes for a while and it was close to 3:00am before I went back to my apartment and got to sleep. I went out with Sally several times, each time repeating having sex in my bedroom. But I got tired of her fairly quickly and stopped calling her.

I got a ride back to New Haven for Thanksgiving break with my roommate George who had an old 49 Dodge with both automatic and manual transmissions. I was welcomed by my mother who told me my father was not well and was upstairs lying in my bed. When I entered my old bedroom I found my father in my bed crying profusely and calling to me, "Jerry! Jerry!" He looked like he was five years older disheveled and had lost at least twenty to thirty pounds since I last saw him three months ago. I was in a state of shock and don't remember clearly how I reacted.

I went to my mother demanding to know why she had not written to me regarding the state of my father's health. We wrote each other every few weeks while I was in Boston. She said she didn't want to upset me and interfere with my school work. She said that my grandfather and Uncle Harry would be here soon to offer support to my father in any way possible.

What she told me about my father's condition was not entirely clear. I remember bits and pieces. Dad had been in a state of depression for the last month. He seldom got out of bed, stopped seeing patients, stopped eating and talked about wanting to die. She had called doctors at Yale New Haven Hospital and they suggested hospitalization and shock treatments. Years ago, during the time I was in the hospital after being run over by a car Dad had gone into a similar state of depression but completely recovered after several months. She said that at that time my grandfather suggested that Dad go into a hospital for shock treatments but she wanted to care for him herself until he recovered. I had no memory of seeing my father for a while after I returned from the hospital in Stroudsburg years ago. I also have no memory of how dad recovered from this most recent depression but he did recover in a few months. At first he stayed close to home, working on some oil paintings he made at the time. I still have one of them that is very precious to me. Soon he started going around looking for a doctor that might need help with his practice. In a few months he started working with a doctor in Ansonia, CT, about 25 miles from New Haven. He never returned to his private practice in New Haven, which was quite successful for many years and paid for my college education.

I felt guilty that I didn't do more to relieve my father from his suffering that he was going through but I simply didn't know what to do or even what to say. But I have no clear memory of my thanksgiving vacation that year in New Haven. We missed the festive Thanksgiving Day dinners that we used to have at Uncle Harry's. I do know that I was aware of depression, the illness, and that it was genetic in character, handed down from generation to generation. I was also aware that someday I might suffer from the same illness, which was a frightful thought. During the vacation my mother took me aside and passed on some information I had not been aware of. This was not the first depression my father suffered. The first depression came in the late 1930's after he had graduated from the University of Michigan and had applied to medical school. The depression with minor hospitalization occurred when he was not accepted to medical school. My mother's mother became psychotic two years after my mother was born and institutionalized for the rest of her life. I never met her or said two words to her. My mother's father didn't speak English at the time and supported my mother and her brother by selling cheap clothing from a push cart around the neighborhood in a small town east of Pittsburg, PA. My mother came home from school to an empty house but found company from neighbors who looked after her. She wanted to go to college but it was financially impossible. After graduating high school she worked as a file clerk. She loved me dearly and felt that it was a miracle I was alive after being run over by a large Buick. One of my father's brothers was prone to depression when he was out of work. He owned a catering company that served meals for TV and movie productions over most of the western part of the country. When he was working he made out quite well but when his job ended he would slump into a depression that lasted for months. Hearing these stories was a shocking experience. I had always thought that I came from a fairly normal family despite my father's idiosyncratic activities. I had considered myself lucky because I heard my friends complain of difficulties and lack of closeness in their families.

In a few days George stopped by to pick me up and we returned to Boston through very heavy traffic on the Mass. Turnpike. As soon as I got back to my room I tried to sort out my thoughts regarding my major course of study. My abilities lie naturally in math and the physical sciences and I enjoyed working in both of these areas. I randomly opened a physics book to a page with a graph showing the orbits of electrons around the nucleus of an atom. I was amazed that mathematics could be used to describe things that were completely invisible to the most powerful microscopes. I had chosen Pre Med as a major almost entirely at the suggestion of my father and felt that being a doctor required communication skills that I simply didn't have at that time.

Without thinking more deeply about the issue I decided to change my major course of study to Physics and continued to work in this area for many years to come. I didn't consider that in later years my interests would change.

Christmas vacation came quickly and I have few memories of the time I spent at home. I know my father's condition improved considerably but he had not started working in Ansonia. It was a great relief to see him up and about. He had gained a fair amount of weight and was in pretty good spirits. I borrowed his car and took Libby to Sleeping Giant Park where we made out like usual. When we were ready to leave I started the car and discovered we had parked in a patch of mud. The tires spun but we didn't move. I have no idea how we got out of this predicament but probably walked to a phone and called a towing company. It was very late when I got home.

I have few memories of spring semester second year. I was dating and going to parties quite a bit, but the only girl I went out with steadily was Jackie, an attractive good natured girl with a nice sense of humor whose parents came from the Netherlands. She was my age and we went to parties and also some concerts that I really enjoyed—Peter, Paul and Mary who were near the height of their popularity, Theodore Bikel whose singing in multiple languages was exceptional and Pete Seeger whose talent and political positions were very satisfying just to name a few.

I had become very comfortable with making out but Jackie had reservations with making love and I respected that. We kept our underwear on and made out until I ejaculated. Jacky went to the Netherlands for the summer and we wrote each other several times.

I returned to New Haven and the cottage for the summer. I started to date Isobel, who lived in the neighborhood. She was fun to be with and we spent a lot of time together. My father was hesitant about my driving into New York, so we took the train and subways to Greenwich Village, which was always a fun place to hang out. Issy, as she liked to be called, was very comfortable with sex. We made love in my father's car and I was careful to use a condom. The possibility of Issy getting pregnant was very scary. I missed her at the end of the summer. She went to college in Virginia and we wrote frequently. I was very comfortable with her emotionally but also wanted a women who had more serious interests.

During the summer I had a job working for Olin Metals Corporation doing projects that involved physics and chemistry. I worked in a lab for a senior scientist with several other full time men. Although the work was not that interesting nor particularly memorable I enjoyed the experience very much. We started out the morning having coffee sitting around telling jokes and relating our sexual experiences. During lunch break we spent the full hour playing Pinochle. The pay was reasonable, $100 per week, more than I ever earned before. Although the job was not academically challenging I enjoyed the friendship that developed between me and the other employees.

My father had fully recovered from his depression and was working comfortably with a doctor in Ansonia. He would pick me up after work and drive out to the cottage to enjoy the lake and fresh country air. I never knew exactly what brought about his depression, his lack of interest in his work or in life itself, but as far as I could tell he was once again his normal self and returned to having his normal ideas and activities.

During my first semester junior year I took the prescribed physics courses and a class in computers. Of course there were no personal computers in 1963. There were large main frames that accepted the Fortran language written on a stack of cards. The course consisted of writing crude programs to solve problems. Unlike standard math, Geometry, Algebra, Calculus, etc. the basic concepts of writing a computer program was very difficult for me to comprehend. I was doing poorly in the course with about a C average when I decided to drop the course. It was the only course I ever dropped at MIT but the difficult experience I had with the course left a lasting impression on me to the present day.

When personal computers came along I stayed away from them as long as I could and after I bought a PC I had various problems with it that required calling for assistance. If at all possible I preferred to deal with business situations by phone or by mail.

On November 23 I was doing homework in the main library when I heard a group of people talking outside the main entrance. Since the noise was disturbing I left the library and listened to what people were saying. "Kennedy has been shot!" "President Kennedy is dead!" I found it hard to believe. My heart was beating faster than normal. I took my books, left the school and went back to the fraternity house as fast as I could. We had a TV in the basement and when I got there fifteen to twenty brothers were watching in total silence as Walter Cronkite repeated the news, "President Kennedy was shot this afternoon while riding in the streets of Dallas in an open motorcade. He was quickly taken to the nearest hospital where he was pronounced dead due to a bullet wound to the back of his head." Cronkite was visibly shaken as he removed his eye glasses and was close to tears. The TV room was quiet as no one knew what to say.

I will remember forever what I did and how I felt the rest of that day and the following day. Dinner in the fraternity house was normal but quiet. It was a Friday night and I had a date with Jackie. Whatever plans we had, we changed them and simply went for a walk. It was a dark dreary night after a thunder storm. We walked in the streets still covered with water. We said very little, occasionally holding hands. We ended up in an apartment that I believe belonged to one of my frat brothers. There was a sofa in an empty room and we made out holding each other closely and kissing passionately.

Then next day I remember spending a lot of time watching TV and following the latest political events. Sunday I had a date with Marg. We had a very cordial relationship spending a lot of time getting to know each other discussing current events, etc. This Sunday we walked along the Charles River. Thick dark clouds were rolling quickly to the East covering the sky. A West wind was blowing briskly. It seemed almost as if the world was soon to come to an end. Although I forgotten the details of our conversation I sensed that we just needed to comfort each other.

Thanksgiving vacation came soon and I got another ride with George to New Haven. Life returned somewhat to normal and I was doing my homework when the song came on the radio that was different. It had a strong beat, strong lyrics and a joyous bouncy feeling. The announcer said it was "A new song by a group called The Beatles from England." They had plans to come to America. I followed popular music very closely at the time and when I heard "I want to hold your hand" I said to myself, "That song will go to #1".

My parents were doing well. My sister was applying to college and later accepted at Wheaton, a small girl's school 40 miles south of Boston. That winter belonged to the Beatles—nationally on the Ed Sullivan Show—and locally their songs filled up the pop music charts from #1 down to #8. It was hard to find a pop station that wasn't playing a Beatles song and "Beatles groups" were popping up all over town playing fraternity parties as well as theaters.

They seemed to be just what the country needed, something to feel good about after the horrible tragedy of Kennedy's death. Dancing to Beatles music was a truly joyous experience. Knowing the words to their early songs came easy. I even had a copy of their first American album, "Meet the Beatles", which I must have played several hundred times.

During intersession a group of guys from the fraternity spent the weekend at Mount Snow. I'm not a very good skier so I took the long, winding, gentle slope down to the bottom. It was fun. The course work got harder.

I went to a lot of parties and my grades slipped below Dean's list. Towards the end of my junior year I began thinking about the future. There was no doubt I wanted to go to graduate school but I did apply for at least one job—with McDonnell Aircraft Corporation in St. Louis. They flew me out for an interview. Things went well and I was offered a job in research. I even interviewed with the Air Force. I applied to the University of Chicago, my first choice, Yale University and the University of Maryland. I was thrilled to be accepted at the University of Chicago. I had visions of myself as an intellectual mingling with the great minds at U of C.

But first there was the summer before senior year, which I spent in Boston working at the Cambridge Electron Accelerator (CEA). I was assigned to the small group that maintained the vacuum system of the accelerator. The work was easy and I had time to read books on Quantum Mechanics. On weekends I went sailing, played tennis, and went to movies and coffee houses.

The highlights of the summer were driving down to Newport, Rhode Island for the Jazz Festival and Folk Festival. Newport is a fairly small town known for the summer homes of the turn of the century very rich and famous. I would guess the population of Newport was about 50,000 people, but during the festivals the population would more than double as music fans jammed the streets. Festival attendance was estimated at

60,000 people with Frank Sinatra at the Jazz Festival and Pete, Paul and Mary at the Folk Festival. After the performance the cars were sitting bumper to bumper for hours and we decided to try to sleep in Mike's car.

Senior year started out well with my grades improving after a dip in junior year. I was still seeing Jackie and writing to Issy. My father was doing well still working in Ansonia and my mother had a break from care taking when my sister went off to Wheaton College.

When I came back to New Haven at Thanksgiving the weather was poor with cold rain and wind. I was running around outside and saw Issy but came down with a cold. Upon returning to MIT the cold got worse and I developed a bad cough along with it. I saw the school doctor and he put me in the infirmary for several days. I tried to keep up with my homework. When I called Jacky she said she wanted to break off our relationship but didn't explain or give any reasons. I was upset and couldn't concentrate for several days. During our Christmas vacation we went to Mount Snow for some more great skiing and when we returned to MIT I concentrated on schoolwork and began to look for another girlfriend.

Eventually I found Arleen. I could melt just looking at her with that thick black hair, large brown eyes and full luscious lips. She had a perfect figure, five foot four inches, very easy going but intelligent. Sometimes I thought I was dreaming when I looked at her. The course load for my last semester was quite demanding—Electric Engineering, Statistical Mechanics, Solid State Physics, Electromagnetic Radiation and Senior Thesis—I worked hard and brought my grades well above those required for Dean's list. But I always looked forward to weekends and seeing Arleen.

I was offered a summer job doing research at NUOS, the Naval Underwater Ordnance Station in Newport and readily accepted. A friend from another fraternity, Barry, also accepted a summer position at NOUS and we shared an apartment. The money was good so I rented a car for the summer.

During my last weekend in Boston I was with Arleen and we wanted to do something different. "Let's go down to Cape Cod." With no car hitchhiking was a good option. Arleen stood on side of the highway while I stepped down out of sight. In less than a minute or two a car stopped and I popped into the car with Arleen. The driver was friendly and in about an hour later he dropped us off on a street in Hyannis. We walked toward the beach and on the way met a guy and started talking. He was going to spend the night with his mother and had a cabin near the beach which he never locked. He asked if we could use a place to stay for the night and when we said yes he explained clearly how to find his cabin. But before we "checked in" we went out to the shore and walked in the moon light for a while, breathing fully the still clear air, captivated by the moon light on the ocean.

The cabin was small but had a good sized sofa that we could lay on and get cozy. We talked for a while between kissing and eventually fell asleep. Later, much later, I stayed in five-star hotels but never felt so wonderful as that night with Arleen, having graduated with honors from MIT, having a summer job in Newport and having been accepted at the U of C for Graduate school. Arleen and I had breakfast in Hyannis and hitched a ride back to Boston.

My parents and sister came up to Boston that weekend for my graduation and I showed them around the campus and the fraternity house. It was a beautiful sunny day; Sailboats were out on the Charles River. Taking pictures in my graduation gown standing on the steps of MIT's main building was a dream come true. My parents were able to take my trunk all packed back to New Haven. I said goodbye to some of the guys in the house and went back to New Haven with my parents, where I packed a suitcase ready to leave for Newport.

NUOS was a large naval station with multiple functions: to carry out research for naval devices was one of them and I worked on several projects while I was there. Improving the capabilities of sonar was another one of them. I don't remember the details of some of the projects but I do remember that they had great tennis courts for workers on the base. Barry and I played every week.

Newport is such a wonderful town. I was very impressed with most of the summer homes of the wealthy that had been transformed into museums. Barry found a steady girlfriend, Carol, rather quickly and spent most of his free time with her. I also found a girlfriend, Tonya, who I saw quite often but also spent time reading and exploring Newport. The National Tennis Museum is located in Newport and we got to see some good matches there. At one point my father and mother came up to visit and enjoyed the tourist attractions including the large summer "cottages".

Once again the highlights of the summer in Newport are the Jazz Festival and the Folk Festival. I invited Arleen up for the Jazz Festival and had a great time. The four of us found a large pot and bought several lobsters to make a fresh boiled lobster dinner. We could walk to the festival avoiding all the traffic of the previous year. I showed her around town and totally enjoyed just being with her. I invited Issy up for the Folk Festival and we also had a wonderful time. On Sunday we drove up to Boston rented a scooter and drove all around the Boston Commons and the Historical District. I can't think of a better place to go to college than Boston.

Toward the end of the summer one of the senior scientists at NUOS took Barry and I for a ride in his sailboat out of Newport Harbor. He told us what a great life it was living and working in Newport, hoping to get us to stay and work permanently at NUOS but both of us had accepted admission to grad school, Barry to Brandeis and I to the University of Chicago. In retrospect staying in New Port would have had many advantages. Barry said goodbye after a wonderful summer and we kept in touch. I returned to New Haven packed my trunk and set out for U of C.

CHAPTER 4
GRADUATE SCHOOL

Chicago is a huge city but I was surprised when I asked for directions to the U of C. I must have thought it was a major landmark but nobody knew how to get there. In any case I found Hyde Park (Home of U. of C.) and registered at the YMCA for a few weeks until I found three roommates to share a great four bedroom apartment in South Shore, about three miles from the campus. Although there was bus service a car would really come in handy and I asked my father if he would pay for a modest car. I had a teaching assistantship which paid for most expenses but I could not afford a car. I looked at several models and really liked the Oldsmobile F-85 that had a standard transmission and a sporty look. My father agreed and I had transportation to school, parties, to downtown, to drive back and forth to New Haven and later to take trips to Canada and Mexico.

My roommates were Warren, John and Ungar. Warren was from California had a BA degree from Berkley and came to the U. of C. to study economics especially with Milton Friedman, his hero. John came from a military family that lived in many cities and came to study International Relations. Ungar was born in Africa and was well educated. I don't remember what he studied. The owners of the three flat building we lived in had the apartment below us on the second floor. They had two children and a very cute, intelligent and sweet small Dachshund. We couldn't ask for nicer more helpful neighbors. We furnished the apartment with the help of the Salvation Army. Our prize piece of furniture was a circular solid oak round table in excellent condition that spread apart to add additional leaves for entertaining.

Since I was the only one with a car I did the weekly shopping. We ate together and shared all expenses. The total grocery bill for the week was usually about $12. We also shared the cooking with each roommate making their favorite dishes.

The U. of C. was on the trimester system with three sessions a year plus an optional summer session. I began taking electro dynamics, mathematical physics and thermodynamics and statistical mechanics. I had been well prepared and got two A's and a B for the first quarter. The professors were all highly respected in their fields. Professor Chandresakar was internationally known for his theoretical studies of solar reactions. However, I didn't feel they were all good teachers for first year students. Chandresakar, who won a Nobel Prize, taught by facing the blackboard, writing one equation after another and mumbling his words so it was difficult to hear. The text he had ordered wasn't available until a month before the end of the course.

Professor Ohme spoke with a heavy German accent. The equations he wrote on the blackboard were highly theoretical so that I had no idea how they applied to electronics in the real world. I requested that he attempt to bring to class some connection between his equations and real world situations. He seemed to move slightly in this direction but I had no further conversations with him.

Over Christmas vacation I drove back to New Haven, visited with the family for a while, saw Issy and went to visit Tonya and Barry who had come to Newport to visit Carol. Barry and Carol had announced their engagement which seemed so natural considering the closeness they developed over the previous summer. Tonya and I made plans to get together again and made love for the first time. We got together at Tonya's home where her mother made a great roast beef dinner.

I found a companion to drive back to Chicago with me and prepared for second semester classes. The qualifying exam was given twice a year and must be passed before students could begin work on their thesis. I had high expectations that I would take the exam second semester but in reality I looked for fun and entertainment and postponed taking the exam until second year. There was an opportunity to go with a group of U. of C. students on a ski trip to Taos New Mexico in late March at break time. It sounded great so I signed up. I had never skied a high mountain.

U. of C. is known for its great Saturday night parties and significant conversation mixed with sexual flirtation. I danced a lot with Betsy at the first party. The sexual attraction was strong and she invited me back to her second floor apartment around midnight. With little conversation we got into bed together and spent hours of passionate love making, which I had never experienced before. Finally I got up and dressed and we walked down the steps to the street. I had an uncomfortable burning feeling in my back, reached behind me and found my hand was bloody. During our time in bed Betsy had been digging her finger nails in my back so forcefully that she had broken the skin in many areas and I was left with blood tricking down my back. I asked her for her name and phone number and we got together for dinner and movies and nights in bed. Later I made plans for September (the U. of C. vacation period) with Warren to travel up the coastal route in California from Los Angeles to San Francisco. Betsy was a senior in the college and was planning on going to San Francisco after her graduation. We talked about meeting in San Francisco and going camping in Yosemite National Park.

In late March between our second and third trimester I followed through with an opportunity to go with a group of students by bus to Taos, New Mexico for a week of skiing. It was too good to pass up. I forgot my plans to take the candidacy exam in June since I was having such a great time. Skiing a large mountain like Taos was a new experience for me since all the skiing I had done was in New England. After three days of skiing I was tired and got together with a couple and went for a walk in the back of the ski lodge. It was delightful walking the trails in the woods until we came to a high bank of ice with no trails. We decided to climb the bank hoping to find hand and foot holes in the ice. After we got more than halfway up the hill I looked down and was terribly frightened. If we fell we would surely be severely injured and continuing up the hill was very difficult. Somehow we reached the top of the bank, warmed our feet and continued on a shallower slope. My heart was beating very quickly and I wondered why I often did such stupid things.

During the week I kept noting a girl I would certainly like to meet. I was too shy to approach her on this trip but an opportunity arose the next fall.

I stayed in Chicago over the summer when I got a scholarship to study Nuclear Physics. In late August I found a passenger going west and we drove out to Bakersfield, California where Warren lived. Stopping at the Grand Canyon we took a day to walk down the Bright Angel Trail but didn't have enough time to reach the bottom and return before dark. The Grand Canyon was the most spectacular sight I had ever seen.

Warren liked to drink and could have several drinks a day on our journey up the coast. I limited my drinking to once a day. We started our trip with a boat ride to Catalina Island over Labor Day weekend, saw the sights of LA and headed north on the coastal route to San Francisco. The drive was very beautiful, Hearst Castle being the most interesting sight. Most memorable in San Francisco was a night club with men dressed completely as females parading around the stage.

We stayed in Warren's old fraternity house while enjoying the sights of San Francisco. We then crossed the bridge and went on up into Wine Tasting Country. It was a wonderful trip. I called Betsy and found that she was no longer interested in going to Yosemite. She had become a flower child. I decided to go alone and stopped to visit her in Haight Ashbury. We had dinner, made love and I was off for Yosemite.

In mid September Yosemite is delightfully uncrowded. I hiked several trails to some quiet views and camped in the valley. It was about a year before I bought my first camera but came back many years later to get the wonderful shots I missed. I found a passenger to go back to Chicago but was not pleased with his fast driving. I had no power over his heavy foot. We returned to Chicago in record time and I was ready to get serious about preparing for the Candidacy exam.

But I screwed up. I saw Marion, the beautiful girl from the Taos trip, in the cafeteria and approached her for a date. I was looking for something different to do and suggested we take a ride to Gary, Indiana where there was a Red Light District. A map of the district with street names and buildings was outlined and appeared in Time magazine a few months ago. A few weeks ago I checked out the district with two of my roommates. We went into one of the bars on the time map but found it looked like an ordinary bar. Eventually the bartender asked us if we were looking for a little action. We said yes and were led to the back of the bar, through one door and out another door. We found ourselves in a totally different atmosphere. This one had five sexy ladies sitting at the bar. As I approached the bar one of them asked if I would like to buy her a drink. It was a rhetorical question. We sat and talked and she went over prices for the different services she offered. She was young and cute, attractive with her hand on my leg. It was difficult to look away but the three of us politely said "Not tonight, Thank You." and went back to Chicago. I have never used the service of a prostitute.

I don't know what made me suggest to Marion that we take a ride to Gary but she said yes and we went to the same bar that I had gone to a few weeks ago. The important thing is that we had a very comfortable conversation driving to Gary and driving back to Chicago. Marion was extremely attractive to me and was a highly intelligent U of C senior. I believe one of her uncle's was a noble prize winner.

On the way back to Chicago I told her a story I had read about a New England couple who were abducted by space aliens. It was a highly convincing article but we agreed not likely accurate. When we got back to her apartment she invited me in, had a drink, kissed goodnight and I left. Sitting in my car I started shaking uncontrollably. I felt a very strong desire to be with her and went back to her apartment. She let me in and eventually we made wonderful love and planned to get together again. I left totally infatuated.

Sometimes I used very poor judgment and let my emotions carry me away. I should have devoted concentrated effort to prepare for the difficult candidacy exam and here I was spending much time with Marion. To make matters worse Marion found another boyfriend in a few months and said goodbye to me just three weeks before the exam.

I failed the exam and felt mildly depressed but planned to study with a fellow graduate student, meeting once a week to go over problems from old tests. In the mean time I made plans to meet Tonya in New York during Christmas vacation. The first thing we did when I got to her apartment was to make love. For the afternoon we went to the Cloisters and the usual museums. We also talked about some long range plans to go to Montreal in June for Expo 67. I then drove to New Haven, saw my parents and Issy. My father was feeling well and still working in Ansonia.

Winter and spring were times of serious study which paid off. I passed the candidacy exam. I then met Tonya in New Haven and we drove to Montreal. I've been to several Expo's but Expo 67 in Montreal was the most memorable of all. I still clearly remember Habitat and the Czech exhibit with the intricate glass exhibits which won the award for the Best of Show. Making love with Tonya was gratifying since I had no sex for the last 6 months while studying for the exam.

Upon returning to Chicago I began the process of finding a thesis advisor. Solid State Physics had appealed to me because it is the basic research that led to microchips which led to personal computer, digital cameras and many other types of micro electronics. I spoke with several professors specializing in Solid State Physics and either they were not taking on new grad students or were not available. I heard about a professor, Dr. Albert Crewe, who was looking for a grad student and we had a long conversation. Dr. Crewe came from England and had worked in the Particle Physics Accelerator Division of Argonne National Labs for several years. He was not only a brilliant physicist but had very good administrative skills. He served as the Director of Argonne Labs for several years and then returned to research pursuing the development of a new type of powerful electron microscope. He explained the project to me, showed me his temporary lab at Argonne and accepted me as a thesis student.

I liked Dr. Crewe's manner very much and the project sounded very interesting. Within a few months his entire lab at Argonne was transferred to the Research Institute at U of C much closer to where I lived. I needed a break from the intense study of the last six months so I took up folk dancing and pursued my interest in photography after borrowing a camera from a friend. Of course I also worked full time learning the basics of Dr. Crewe's new approach to electron microscopy and became friends with three of his other new grad students.

A few months later I met a girl who was a grad student in chemistry at U. of C. at a lecture on campus. We both found the lecture boring and went to a folk dance nearby. When I took her home she asked when I would see her again which seemed rather forward to me. Janet was of course highly intelligent although not especially attractive. She lived in Hyde Park and her parents lived a few miles away in South Shore. We started dating. Every Friday night we went to her parents for dinner and an evening playing bridge. We made love regularly but frequently had arguments which usually ended up with love making.

After understanding the basics of Crewe's novel electron microscope design I was assigned the project of modifying the microscope to make electron holograms, a technically difficult project which had never been done before. Without going into details the project had been explored theoretically by Meir at IBM about fifteen years before. At first progress went very slowly with my working well into the evening.

After more than half a year Janet and I decided to take a camping trip to Banff National Park and Lake Louise. The long drive was well worth the time. Lake Louise remains one of the most spectacularly beautiful areas I've ever visited. We camped in Banff National Park which was practically deserted except for a bear that roamed around looking for food. Lake Louise has a magical blue green color due to the melting glacier runoff that fed into the lake. Hiking up into the hills above Lake Louise was a wonderful experience. We also drove up to Jasper National Park which is more barren and isolated.

After returning to Chicago we learned that we had been away during the infamous Chicago riots during the Democratic Convention that left many protestors injured. It was an embarrassment for Mayor Daley and his police. About that time Dr. Crewe's grad students went to Jimmy's, a favorite bar for U. of C. grad students. After we had a few beers the TV was showing video reports from Kent state College where four undergrad protestors were shot and killed by Army soldiers called in to restore order. My mind shifted from microscope talk to the tragedy that was unfolding across the country. I put my project on hold and went out into the street. I went to a rally in Grant Park, a demonstration in favor of the Chicago 7 and most memorable the joining of a group of 50,000 people each carrying a lit candle in an evening parade down Michigan Avenue. We handed out flyers and talked to people in the streets about the need to end the Vietnam War.

I had bought a Nikkormat Camera from Hong Kong and shot a number of rolls of black and white film around Hyde Park which I developed in my bathroom and was pleased with the results. I had taken the camera to Expo 67 and also began shooting portraits. Photography was to become my most satisfying activity. Back to work at the lab I had some equipment that could potentially make electron holograms but the brightness of the image was not sufficient to take a photograph with normal film and camera. To solve this problem I consulted with Zenith Corporation who made a specially designed fiber optic faceplate with phosphorescent coating that glowed when it was hit by an electron.

During the winter I was driving with Janet to her parents as usual on a Friday night and I noticed she was sobbing somewhat softly. Eventually I inquired what she was crying about. I don't remember the exact words she said but it was something like "I think it's time we decided to get married." I had a soft spot for any person or any animal that was hurt or in pain. I once had a cat that escaped out our back door and we searched the neighboring blocks for hours without finding him. I was sad for days and left the door opened for him to return. About four days later he wandered in, in good condition in any case at this time in an attempt to stop her pain I said to Janet "Okay, let's get married." This was not a well thought out decision. She was instantly overjoyed and we told her parents the good news. It's amazing how I was bright enough to construct the world's first electron hologram but not smart enough to say "Why don't we discuss the situation openly."

Janet wanted a March wedding. I wanted a June wedding. Janet won. I let my parents know about our decision and my father called a week later letting me know that he wanted to speak with me in person. Since I had last seen my parents they had moved to Beaver Falls, Pennsylvania where my father got a job in the Emergency Room of the local hospital.

They lived on the outskirts of town. I took a plane to Beaver Falls with a physics book to study along the way. The purpose of my father's wanting to talk to me was to ask a large number of questions about Janet and how we got along together. Janet could be obstinate and would fight to get her way. My father had pretty much made up his mind that she was not for me and had hoped to persuade me not to marry her. My mother pretty much sat by the sidelines without expressing herself. She seemed to feel that if I really cared about Janet, really loved her, everything would be fine. I was able to answer the first few questions my father asked but eventually the questions got too deep to answer fully and the truth was I had ambivalent feelings about the wedding and simply told myself I'd do my best to make it work.

My father became very anxious when he saw he could not change my mind and my mother and I went with him to see a psychiatrist that he had seen before. The psychiatrist saw my father privately and talked to my mother asking if she thought my father would be okay. She told me not to worry and to do what I thought was best.

I felt uneasy but returned to Chicago to continue work on my thesis. I had little to do with the wedding planning. Janet and I had decided not to go away after the marriage but to take several days off playing tourists in downtown Chicago spending a few nights in the Sheraton Hotel. We planned a "Honeymoon" in September driving to Mexico visiting Mexico City and a lot of the neighboring towns around the capital.

My parents drove out to Chicago for the wedding and the dinner the night before the wedding. My father seemed well and in good spirits. The wedding took place in a south shore hotel. Most of the guests were on the side of Janet's family. It was basically a standard reformed wedding. The best man was my best friend from high school. I don't recall my friends having a bachelor's party for me on the Friday before my wedding. Instead I remember going folk dancing by myself and meeting a woman who invited me to her apartment after the dance where we made satisfying love. This incident should have given me a clue to future events.

To get back to my thesis I picked up the fiber optic face plate that Zenith had fabricated and installed it in my holographic microscope. I designed and built a special camera that took photos on the outer surface of the faceplate that was lit up by electrons striking the inner surface of the faceplate. Looking at the prints from the negatives for the first time I saw a sharp set of black and white lines (called fringes) that were the beginning of an electron hologram. My heart started beating as I couldn't believe everything was working just as predicted. After three years we were beginning to get results.

A few months before the wedding one of my roommates invited a friend to visit after dinner. We sat around in the living room listening to music and Mary asked if anyone wanted to smoke a joint. I had never smoked before but decided to try it. It was a very pleasant experience. The music playing had a heightened melody. I felt very relaxed and silly and started giggling for more than an hour. I could not concentrate on homework for the rest of the evening. Over a year later, after Janet and I were married, we were invited to spend an evening with friends in South Shore. John worked in advertising and Betty had just given birth to a baby girl. After some small talk John asked if we wanted to smoke a joint. I said "Yes", Janet said, "No." I took deep inhalations impatient to experience that relaxed feeling that I had gotten the first time I smoked.

Instead after about ten minutes I felt a very disturbing and frightening sensation of "going inside my head". Trapped inside an inner world and not being able to get out. The outside world looked grossly distorted and time seemed to slow down. The people in the room looked as if they were wearing masks. I had difficulty speaking almost like I was in a different world. The clock hands hardly moved. Betty made coffee and eventually I returned to my normal state of mind. About 3 o'clock in the morning I felt very erotic and woke Janet to make love.

Because the pot experience was so frightening I did some research on its affects. What I found was even more frightening. Known as a bad trip, such an experience was known to unlock a future possible psychosis. During the following few months that feeling of "getting trapped inside my head" recurred several times but only for about 10 seconds. These events were called flashbacks.

The details of making an electron hologram are too involved to discuss here but this first part of my thesis was a great success. However, there was more work to do. Lenses are used to make these holograms and they introduce "aberrations" in the final image. The second part of my thesis was to show that these aberrations could be "corrected" giving a sharper more clear image.

Janet and I planned a vacation to England, Wales and Scotland with her friends Bill and Joan in early April. I felt a little guilty for leaving my work but we drove from Chicago to Beaver Falls to visit my parents on the way to Kennedy airport. That night it started to snow but we decided to make the drive anyway. A blizzard developed that followed us all the way to New York. The plane for London was due to leave at 8:00pm but we didn't get to Kennedy until close to midnight. TWA put us up overnight and we took the first plane out in the morning and met her friends in London. After a harrowing beginning the trip was a lot of fun, mostly visiting old castles and churches. I liked the ruggedness of Wales, the mystery of Stonehenge and the history of the Cambridge home of Isaac Newton.

Not long after returning to Chicago Dr. Crewe told us we were going to the annual EMSA (Electron Microscopy Society of America) meeting in Houston and to prepare a ten minute talk. By the time we left for Houston I had made the first two beam Fresnel Electron Holograms in the world. Of course I did not do it alone. Dr. Crewe had secured the grant to pay for the research and was always available when a problem came up that I couldn't deal with.

Janet came with us to Houston. My talk was smooth and well received and we had some time to visit the city.

In the fall we planned a trip east again visiting my parents and driving up to Boston to visit MIT and the old Fraternity. By the time we got back I was exhausted. Faye called that night and said she had a surprise for us—she was engaged and wanted us to meet her fiancé. She came over with David looking very happy and introduced him as a business man from California. They had gone to Beaver Falls while Janet and I were out east and they had visited my parents where David announced his intention to marry Faye. In addition he found out a lot of information regarding a "conflict" between my father and I that had recently occurred. He seemed to be quite successful and affluent. They had gone shopping in Highland Park an affluent suburb of Chicago and picked out a very nice home to live in. It seemed as if too much was happening too quickly but when David informed me that he wanted to go back to Beaver Falls with Faye and I so that I could resolve any differences between my father and I, I accepted him as an ally and we planned to leave Chicago in four days. It's a ten hour drive. We arrived in Beaver Falls on Friday night. My parents liked and respected David very much. But my mother sensed that he was not an especially warm person to be around. He never hugged her.

The next day my father and I sat down for a heated discussion too complex to go into but we eventually reached a reconciliation. David said he had business in Chicago and took an early Sunday flight back to Chicago. Faye and I drove back to Chicago arriving early Sunday night. A few hours later Faye called and in a very panicky voice told me that all her money was gone. All her checking, all her savings, all her jewelry, etc were gone. She had only the cash left in her wallet. David, who had a key to her apartment, was gone and never seen again. He had convinced Faye to loan him money until he went back to California. The money would be used for a down payment on their new home. The next morning I went with Faye to the FBI office downtown to report the event. We got little sympathy from the FBI agent who said that "This happens frequently and such conmen are seldom caught. Forget it!"

My father who did embrace David with open arms set about on a path to track David down. From police in California he found out that David was a very active conman in California. He got David's real name and found that he had spent time in jail. But the search was futile. My sister asked to borrow some money from my father and planned a Caribbean cruise. I attempted to concentrate on having a talk to give in August at the annual EMSA Conference this year in Boston but all the hectic events of the last year left me exhausted, anxious and depressed. When I saw that I wasn't functioning at what I thought to be my normal level I asked friends for the name of a good psychiatrist. The man I selected was about 35 years old had done his training at the University of Chicago, had an office in downtown Chicago and I believe that he practiced Standard Freudian Psychiatry. His method was to have me talk about whatever came into my mind and he made occasional comments. I saw him regularly twice a week for about a year. During that time overall I got disturbingly worse. Practically the only session I remember with Dr. Kaplan was describing to him all the times I would go to Dr. Crewe's office and talk with his secretary Rose Marie, a very pretty middle aged women who seemed willing to listen to the difficulties I was having. I described how compassionate and how knowledgeable she seemed to be as well as attractive. When I finished my description Dr. Kaplan said "I'd be surprised if you didn't have any sexual fantasies about her." "Yes of course I had." "That's what you repressed" he responded. It was obvious to me that I was sexually repressed at this time but was simply unable to respond sexually in the positive way I had during the last eight years. I was under pressure during that time to find a college position or take a post doctoral research position.

Janet drove us to Boston and the EMSA meeting and as usual we stopped at my parent's home in Beaver Falls. Unexpectedly I found my father very anxious and depressed without understanding what caused this incident. He tried his best to be good company and behave normally but I could easily sense the turmoil that he was going through. I not only felt helpless to offer him support but my own anxiety and fear became enhanced.

We stopped at Cornell University and visited the electron microscope lab of Professor Seigel who had offered me a post doctoral position. He showed me around his lab of which he was very proud and asked me to give a short talk on my thesis work. I found it almost impossible to concentrate on the talk. I was shaking slightly and thinking constantly about my father's condition. I knew he had recovered in short time from previous depressions but that didn't stop my fear and worry. Dr Seigel's lab did not look appealing to me after spending four years in Dr. Crewe's lab. I was in physical pain and psychic distress.

We left Cornell the following morning and went on to Boston. My condition became worse. I was in a totally indecisive state to go ahead and present my talk in this condition or to cancel the presentation due to illness. My fellow grad students offered encouragement and I practiced what I had gone through thoroughly before leaving Chicago.

Finally I gave the talk. I was sweating, in pain and felt totally out of control. When the talk was finished I got into my bathing suit and went to the hotel whirlpool in hope of relaxing. It didn't work. I went to our room and collapsed in our bed. A doctor was called and gave me a shot. I thought it was a tranquilizer but I didn't really know. We decided to leave Boston the next morning for Chicago. I lay in the backseat trying to figure out how I got into this situation.

Both my thesis papers were finished by early fall and submitted to the journal Optik although I lost confidence in what I had done and become even more anxiety ridden. The papers were very well done and published in a few months without corrections. During this time I had anxiety attacks where an event would trigger rapid heart beating that frightened me even more. I followed an instinct to run away and eventually I would calm down.

In mid fall I had only one major responsibility before getting my Ph.D.—defending my thesis before a committee of U of C professors. The professors were interested in my talk and treated me kindly. The defense was basically a done deal. I was anxious but spoke reasonably well.

However, my mental condition deteriorated. I wouldn't go out to a restaurant and was even fearful of leaving our apartment. I stayed inside and started oil painting, attempting an abstract composition. When I did go outside for a while I became frightened after several blocks and returned home. Eventually I couldn't walk more than two blocks from our apartment. I stopped seeing Dr. Kaplan and notified my parents of my condition.

It seemed obvious that I would not be able to accept Professor Seigel's offer for a post doc at Cornell. Dr. Crewe had offered to help me get a post doc at Cal Tech working on a miniature version of his microscope design that would be taken to Mars to study the microscopic features of the planet. I did not feel well enough to consider such a position.

Finally a post doc position was available in Dr. Collins lab at Northwestern University. Janet drove me for an interview and although I hardly knew what I was saying Dr. Collins offered me the position. Dr. Collins was doing research on crystal defects with a conventional transmission electron microscope. I had grave doubts that I could handle the position.

My parents recommended I call Dr. Silverman, my father's psychiatrist. Dr. Silverman said he understood my condition and strongly recommended that I see Dr. Krainis in downtown Chicago. Dr. Krainis was about seventy years old and had written a large book that had become the standard text for treating mental illness.

Since I couldn't drive, Janet drove me to see Dr. Krainis where I started complaining about my condition. His first words to me were "You're going to be okay! You will recover." He gave me three medications to take: Marplan, an anti-depressant, Mellaril, an anti-anxiety agent and Doriden, a sleeping pill. He then asked if I had a job. I said I had accepted a post doc position at Northwestern University with Professor Collins. He spoke to me very seriously saying "I want you to promise me you will go to work every day no matter how you feel." I had doubts that I could follow through but gave him my word I would take the job.

CHAPTER 5
FIRST DEPRESSION

I never got my degree in person. Faye had a friend Bill, a very jovial guy from Israel, who was about my age. I had decided after much anguish to separate from Janet. Bill offered to drive us to Beaver Falls. At first I was afraid to go more than a few blocks from their home. I borrowed my father's bicycle and would take a ride each day going a little further. I received my Ph.D. while staying at my parents home and accepting their care for me making all my meals and listening to my tales of worry and hopelessness. My father, who had been seriously depressed during my visit in August was in a good mood and tried to offer me understanding and compassion.

"Bipolar-Mind"—Confusion, reeds near shore

Faye left for her cruise to the Caribbean. When she returned we made plans for the near future. I would move in with Faye until I was ready to get my own apartment. The drive to Northwestern was about ten miles. Difficult for me, but not impossible. The month of January was very difficult. Concentrating on any work, learning to use the transmission microscope was also not easy. I never went out at night. It was difficult making a simple decision. I had no life besides work which I didn't like.

One night Faye was planning on going to a "singles dance" and insisted I go with her to get me out of the apartment. I don't remember talking with anyone at the dance. Faye danced with several men and met Barry who was interested in going out with her. Faye was receptive and they started dating steadily. Barry was recently divorced, got depressed and was helped by a friend who took him to the Ted Liss Acting School where he met new people and regained his interest in life. Barry offered to help me by taking me to the Ted Liss Acting School.

Upon entering the school I felt like I was in a different world away from cold scientific equipment and into a warm world of young people training their voices and acting skills. Ted offered me a monologue to prepare for the following week—Tom's monologue at the beginning of "Glass Menagerie". I now had something to do at night. As I walked across the stage the next week and faced the audience of students I thought I would I die on the spot but words started coming out and I was still alive. I can remember that monologue forty years later.

It wasn't long before I began to enjoy doing scenes with a partner as well as monologues. I had something to look forward to, reading plays every week. After months of practice I was advanced to the next higher class.

By the end of March I was ready to get my own apartment. I found a sunny one bedroom third floor walk up close to shopping, parks and midway between Northwestern and the Ted Liss School. Barry and Faye helped me move furniture and other belongings from the old apartment I shared with Janet. The decision to divorce Janet was complex and painful. We spoke a lot, mostly regarding details of the divorce. It seemed the right thing to do.

During this time and for some time to come it was clear that I was clinically depressed. I joined a group called "Recovery" to gain insight as to how I might relieve many of the physical pains that go along with depression. The basic approach of recovery was to say to ourselves "The symptoms of pain and anxiety that I feel are uncomfortable but not dangerous." I had limited success with this approach. One of my symptoms was chest pain that I interpreted as a heart problem. The pain would get worse when I ran. I went to a heart specialist who attached a recorder to my chest that recorded heart functioning continuously. No heart problems were recorded. Eventually I learned that assorted medical and emotional symptoms were related to my depressive illness. I also started reading Dr. Krainis' soft cover book, "Help for the Depressed" underlining all the sections that seemed to apply to me. I took walks through the neighboring parks taking colored pictures of the sunsets.

During our marriage I had remained faithful to Janet but in retrospect I was only punishing myself. Approaching new women was difficult at first. I went out with a young woman, Pat, from Recovery. She was a virgin. I did not see her very long. I met Eileen at a singles group. She was friendly, easy to get along with and had a good sense of humor. She enjoyed sex. I was improving. Our divorce was arranged by a lawyer friend of Janet's family. I did not have to appear in court. I guess it was called a no fault divorce. We divided mutual property and I had no financial responsibility. I never saw her again although I knew she accepted a post doctoral research position at the University of Washington and then took a job with IBM in Stanford.

The biggest event I took part in before our formal divorce was the 25 mile walk for Israel. Several professors at Northwestern sponsored me. We left at 7:30am, made a circle around the north side of the city and returned to the Jewish Community Center. When we completed walking my feet were very sore but I felt it was necessary to accept challenges to overcome my basically depressed state.

Every summer Ted arranged to bring about thirty of his students to an actor's camp in central Wisconsin. I went with Eileen and Faye and Barry who were married back in April in a short ceremony in the Rabbi's Study. My parents did not attend. There was ample recreation as well as daily rehearsals. I was in the chorus for "Seven Brides for Seven Brothers". We had just seven days to put the entire show together and then we performed it for all the camp members. I was making progress in acting school and also began to take "head shots" of students who were preparing to look for modeling and acting jobs. It wasn't for the money. I really enjoyed photography.

Downstairs from my apartment lived a young couple I met who were very friendly and we frequently had dinner together. Mike and Susie were congenial to have as neighbors and we really enjoyed the time we spent together. They knew a woman who was a teacher that they thought I might enjoy meeting. She was Italian and came from family of four girls and two boys. When I called her she invited me to come out to her home where we played tennis in the backyard. I was instantly attracted to her and we started going out together. She was not only very attractive but lively and emotional. A month after we met I asked her to move in with me. She was everything Janet was not. Our first project was to completely remodel the apartment.

In the meantime my post doc with Professor Collins expired in December 72 and I had no job. Andrea worked part time teaching middle school. I was offered another post doc at Northwestern with Professor Edelstein in the Department of Chemical Engineering and Astronautical Sciences. The department may have had a fancy name but the project I worked on was totally boring—measuring the size of molecular clusters by means of electron diffraction. But Professor Edelstein was younger and more communicative than Professor Collins. I also enjoyed spending time with the glass blower and the machinist in the department.

My cognitive ability improved considerably along with my ability to focus and I built an apparatus that could lower the air pressure inside a chamber to 10^{-8} mm and could be used to take electron diffraction pictures of molecular clusters but while Professor Edelstein was away at conferences I got into a silly mood and painted the apparatus I built with blue and green paint and labeled it "Super Mucket". Professor Edelstein did not see the humor in my paint job and withheld my final month's salary.

Being with Andrea was a pleasure whether it was eating, dancing, walking or working on the remodeling project. When summer came we went to actor's camp again and heard a lecture by a Gestalt Therapist who gave us some examples of the methods used in this form of therapy. I felt the need for work in this area and began therapy with Gestalt Therapist Charlotte Rosner when we returned to Chicago. I had developed areas of tension in my neck and shoulders that were very annoying. When I heard an ad on the radio for a yoga center not far from where I lived. I went to a class and found it relaxing and helpful in dealing with my tension. It became a discipline two or three days a week of class plus some work at home. I practiced and later taught Yoga classes for thirty years and feel it has contributed significantly to my physical wellbeing. In my final session with Dr. Krainis he discontinued my medication and strongly urged me to actively pursue a career. I prepared a good resume for a teaching job and included letters of recommendation and transcripts of my college and grad school work. I was offered interviews at out of state colleges—The University of Arkansas and the University of Northern Colorado—but no job offers. It was local colleges and universities that offered me part time jobs. In most cases I accepted the part time jobs even though I could not make a living from them and accepted jobs outside of teaching to make ends meet. From the end of the two post docs I held for the next four years my memory is somewhat poor as to the sequence of jobs I held, my activities, my friends, my women, etc.

Although I was basically depressed during most of this time there were periods when normal feelings surfaced and I actually felt quite good. I will attempt to outline the diversity, the many jobs, therapies, activities, and women I used to put my feelings together and become whole again.

Gestalt Therapy was basically developed by Fritz Perls in Esalen, California. Examples of his technique were found in his book "In and Out the Garbage the Pail". His approach offered an alternative to Freudian therapy. In my work with Charlotte Rosner I dealt with unfinished issues with my father and current issues with Andrea. Overall the approach attempts to improve methods of communication as well as finding ways to lead a more satisfying life.

After about two years Charlotte recommended that I switch therapists to her husband, Richard, who was the leader of the Gestalt Therapists in the Chicago area. Richard was highly unconventional in his approach to therapy. I worked with him in a small group once a week. We read one of Carlos Casteneda's books and looked for comparisons between Casteneda's writings and Gestalt therapy. We also did mutual nude massage. I enjoyed massage, built a massage table and shared massage with a number of friends.

After a year of working with Richard I was feeling better and made a commitment to learning Gestalt therapy techniques. I was in a group of about ten people of varying ages and a group leader that alternated from a staff of about eight well trained therapists. Near the end of the first year we were required to write a paper that answered a number of questions about Gestalt. I worked hard on the paper using Fritz Perls as a reference. About six weeks after turning my paper in it still had not been returned. I complained to my group leader but was not satisfied with her response. I abandoned my commitment to the further learning of Gestalt techniques but continued to use many of them that I learned for many years to come.

I began practicing Yoga in 1973 at the Sivananda Yoga Center in Chicago. In good weather I would bike to the center. The Chicago Center was one of many centers established around the world by Swami Vishnu who was one of the few Swami's who brought Yoga from India to the west. The Shivananda teachers were well trained leading the students through the same postures and breathing exercises for 1 ½ hours in each class. Each student was taught to progress at their own level. After about half a year I was able to do the head stand and other advanced postures. Prior to Yoga I had done weight lifting and running for exercise. Yoga was more effective at reducing the chronic tension I had developed over the last three years.

We were taught that yoga did not consist strictly of postures but also proper diet, proper breathing and proper meditation. I gave up eating red meat which had been a staple in my diet until I turned 30. At first the transition was difficult but eventually I felt better on a mostly vegetarian diet. I practiced breathing exercises and eventually my nostrils were clearer and I stopped getting the two colds a year I was used to catching. In the summer of 1977 I drove to Val-Morin, Canada to take the six week Shivananda teachers training course taught by Swami Vishnu. We did two one and a half hour sessions of proper postures and had three hours of lectures every day. The lectures were mostly at odds with Western Science and I frequently disagreed with Swami Vishnu's teachings of the "Bhagavad-gita, Chakras", reincarnation, celibacy and other assorted Hindu concepts. There were eleven Ph.D.'s in our class of 110 students but I was the most argumentative. Eventually I went to Swami Vishnu's private residence and knocked on his door. He listened to my difficulty accepting the details of his lectures after studying ten years of employing the scientific method but he got angry and said "This is what I teach here. You don't like it, you can leave." During the summer of 1977 there was considerable conflict between Swami Vishnu and the Mahareshi Mahesh Yogi who was claiming that his students could levitate. There was media coverage at Val-Morin where Swami Vishnu claimed levitating by meditating was impossible.

The vegetarian diet at the camp became very monotonous after a few weeks and I joined a group of students who drove to a nearby restaurant for a chicken dinner. Going six weeks without sex was also difficult but I survived. A group of about twenty students took a vow of chastity. But after the class was over I bet most of them returned to their normal habits. After six weeks teaching certificates were handed out in a joyous ceremony and I started teaching at the center in Chicago a few weeks after returning home.

Andrea was a bright light in my life for more than a year. When the owners of the building we lived in saw the bright orange, green and blue colors we used to paint our apartment they were furious and gave us notice to leave when our lease expired. I moved to a first floor apartment less than a mile away. Andrea moved to a high rise building downtown. She evidently was satisfied with our relationship even though I had been suffering symptoms of depression. She gave me an ultimatum: commitment to marriage in one month or our relationship would be over. The decision weighed heavy on me. I had been with her over the last year and a half and we couldn't refrain from making love in her apartment. She later came to me with her dilemma. She was pregnant.

My assets were very low and I had no prospects for a permanent job. Marriage at this time made no sense. I left her pregnancy condition up to her. She told me she had sex in a one night stand a few months ago. Still I felt terrible. I was very attracted to her and liked the emotional relationship we had much more than that with Janet. I retreated to my new apartment, did a lot of Yoga, read poetry, especially the "Love song of J. Alfred Prufrock", which I memorized. Finally with the help of Richard, my therapist at the time, I said no to Andrea.

Looking through Chicago magazine I saw a notice for a folk dancing group that met once a week in a nearby grade school. The warm welcome I got and the acceptance of the group opened up a whole new social outlet for me and I became a regular dancer attending two or three dances a week.

Out of the basic need to pay my bills I answered an ad in a local newspaper for a janitor at the Orchard Center for Mental Health. I explained my position as an unemployed Ph.D. looking for a teaching position who needed temporary work. The director of the agency had empathy for me and I was hired. When I got home at first I cried. Here I was just three years after working at the very forefront of electron microscopy and electron holography with one of the foremost professors in the field in one of the greatest universities in the country and I was beginning work scrubbing hallways, vacuuming carpets and mowing the lawn.

I had never really embraced Judiasm as my religion. I did work hard to say the prayers at my bar mitzvah and give "Now I am a Man" speech. I enjoyed the party with my friends and relatives very much. Then I went on for another year of Hebrew school. One of the young Hebrew school teachers recognized my potential and encouraged me to study to become a Rabbi. "All the great teachers are in the Bible" he said. But it was too late. I had already embraced science as the bearer of truth and would argue for science against all other "truths". But when I had the chance I joined a group of Jewish men and women my age in regularly attending Saturday morning services. I liked the singing and feeling of belonging.

At services I met Carol—a would be artist. I was very impressed with her drawings and still have one she made for me but even more I enjoyed making love with her. I liked the touch of her skin and the way she moved gently.

During this time I took up cooking, finding exotic recipes and cooking them for company. There was much satisfaction in creating dishes better than those found in restaurants.

CHAPTER 6

RECOVERY

After a while I got to know some of the social workers in the agency especially Mary who worked in a large playroom with six mentally retarded patients from eighteen to thirty-one years old. Each patient had a different diagnosis and prognosis but Mary treated them all with tenderness compassion and humor. She also had 5 children of her own. I loved our daily conversations. During the last year I had some autumn color photos enlarged and framed. We hung them in the hallways of Orchard Center. I actually began to feel comfortable in my job as janitor. Of course I had developed many other interests in the last few years.

The Director of the agency saw that I was beginning to like being a janitor too much when I should be looking for a teaching position. I regularly, meticulously vacuumed his office. Yet he called me in a few minutes later and found a small wad of paper under his desk. He told me the quality of my work was deteriorating and he would have to fire me. Before I had a chance to feel really badly he explained that I would be able to collect unemployment insurance if I was fired. He was just trying to help me out. I collected unemployment.

I continued sending out resumes with no results. But I did find a photographer nearby who needed a black and white printer for his business I had a lot of experience printing black and white scenics and head shots in the dark room of the northwestern university basement and did a good job for him.

Somehow, I don't remember how, I got a one year teaching position in physics that was available at Elmhurst College about 25 miles from my apartment. Basically a protestant school Elmhurst had a small but pretty campus. I taught basic physics, modern physics, physical science and electron microscopy techniques. I kept an eye on Penny, a very bright high school senior who was placed in the freshman physics class at Elmhurst.

Somehow I found a friend to carpool with. It not only made the drive pleasant but George and I became quite close. We shared our anxiety problems and started a running program twice a week. Each time we ran we would start from a different location and eventually went past the point of pain to running more than an hour at a time. Although Penny was only about half my age I dated her for a while after second semester was over and found her very refreshing.

During the second semester I heard from an old friend in my post-doc days at Northwestern University. Stan had gotten a research job with 3M Company and moved to Minneapolis where he was quite happy. His plan for me and another friend of his was to take a train up to Minneapolis where he would meet us with his car and ride straight through to the North entrance to Yellowstone National Park.

Considering that I was still in a somewhat depressed state the trip was ambitious for me but I went anyway. During the whole length of the trip to the park I lay in the back seat of the car but could not sleep. We made a stop on the western plains after sunrise. The air was crisp and clear. A feeling of fear overcame me similar to the feeling I had over four years ago when I tried to go more than two blocks from my apartment. I sought refuge from this fear by getting into Stan's car. I worried that I was not in a frame of mind to enjoy this trip but continued on. We entered Yellowstone Park from the north entrance where the snow had just been plowed a week before. The snow banks were about fifteen feet high.

At this time in early June the park was practically empty. We drove down to a lower elevation and rented a cabin. My camera was somewhat therapeutic. When I concentrated on framing a scene my sense of fear would temporarily dissipate. Without the camera I had uncontrollable feelings of wanting to leave Yellowstone and go back to the soothing woods of the Midwest but we went to Yellowstone Falls, the geyser and the thermal areas where heated water came out to the surface and into rivers and spilled out over the multi colored rocks. Some of my pictures came out better than I expected but I didn't make a very good companion because my depressive thoughts were so pervasive.

Finally Stan drove down to the local train station and put the two of us on a train back to Chicago. He drove on to Grand Teton National Park. Once I was on the train my mood improved. I had a summer job teaching physics at North Park College and I prepared an outline and reviewed some basic topics. During the previous year I had joined a group from the local temple in forming a bridge club playing once a week. We discovered that we liked camping at state parks in Illinois, Wisconsin, Michigan and Indiana. Every other week we packed our gear and got a good supply of sirloin steaks, baking potatoes, fruits and vegetables. Cooking over an open fire was very satisfying to me, reminiscent of my Boy Scout years and of course in our spare time we got several bridge games going. At this point in my life the local state parks were very satisfying even though an adventure to Yellowstone was too much for me to handle.

The summer physics class was very enjoyable. The students came mostly from the University of Illinois, had goals of having a professional career and were willing to work on the course material. My experience at North Park was much more satisfying than that at Elmhurst so that I looked forward to future full time teaching assignments.

About this time I was contacted by a friend that I knew while doing post doctoral research at northwestern. He told me that a number of women at the church he belonged to got together and formed a "women's group". He asked me if I would be interested in forming a "men's group" that would meet one night a week in the same church. The details of meeting and the organization of the group were to be determined. I was interested in the idea and became a charter member—ten men with no leader. We sat in a circle and each person in turn talked about his most significant feelings and events in his current life. Other members then had the opportunity to offer support and encouragement to the first person. A majority of the initial members were associated with academics and an atmosphere of courtesy and empathy developed rather quickly.

I became especially close with two of the group members and we met together to share further details in our lives. Three of us decided to rent an apartment together in the spring of 1977.

During that time I was teaching a Physics class at Loyola University (Chicago) with an enrolment of over seventy students. It was the largest class I ever taught. The students were practically all pre-med or pre-dent and very compatible. I wanted to establish a somewhat easy going atmosphere in the class and began by asking if anybody knew any good jokes. I got one response at the beginning of the class. He opened with some very funny jokes that were somewhat risqué. Some of the students seemed to think that I didn't know very much about physics. I came in the next day with a lecture based on the meaning of the Schroedinger Equation in the field of Quantum Mechanics. With my respect restored it turned out to be the best part time class I ever taught. I felt on par with two of the other physics teachers in the department and we had interesting conversations on physics and astronomy.

While I was teaching at Loyola a notice came to the physics department that St. Xavier College on the south side of the city was looking for a physics teacher that could also develop an astronomy program as well as upgrade the physics laboratory. Although I had never taken an astronomy class I convinced the interviewers that I had a strong background in astronomy based on my building and using an 8″ telescope and could teach the subject at the level that would be expected.

CHAPTER 7

TEACHING COLLEGE

After 4 years without a full time job I finally got a position as assistant professor of Physics at St. Xavier College. I was thrilled. When I returned from Val Morin with my Yoga teachers certificate I went to St. Xavier and talked for a while with the science department chairman. I got right to work straightening out the remains of the physics lab which had been taught by part time teachers. I made a list of equipment we would need as well as two telescopes for the astronomy class: a Celestron 8" and a Questar 3½" both with good motor drives. I had a very reasonable budget and looked forward to getting all the equipment we would need. Of course I now made my job #1 priority but continued with a number of activities I had gotten into prior to this current position. I had a lot to give in teaching science. My voice and diction and acting training, although satisfying, lasted only somewhat over three years. It made sense to continue in the teaching field. I had an intuitive feeling for science which I did not have for acting. I showed slides of the human side of Einstein, his family, his interests in sailing and playing the violin and some of his eccentricities.

I had discontinued seeing Dr. Krainis somewhere in 1974 and stopped taking the medication he prescribed with his permission. I discontinued Gestalt workshops after my 20 page assigned paper was never returned. Teaching Yoga remained a wonderful way to keep my body in shape and my mind at peace. George and I remained friends for a while until his interests turned to ultraorthodox Judaism and he married a woman with four children. My good friend, Jack, from the men's group divorced his wife and married a woman Pastor. He died of colon cancer two years later. I also taught physics, math and holography part time at several local colleges and junior colleges.

My father had run into some conflicts at the hospital where he was working in the emergency room. I never learned any of the details but he left the hospital and moved to Harrisburg. From there he found two jobs in two different hospitals in the Scranton area which he knew very well from his early years. This excessive responsibility and lack of sleep led me to conclude he was relatively high (manic) and would eventually crash.

During the summer of '78, a year after teaching at St. Xavier, I took a raft trip down the Yampa and Green Rivers in Utah. I was in great shape from running and Yoga. The other rafters were interesting and made good company. The guides were excellent at handling the rafts and cooking terrific meals. The trip lasted six days and my feelings (unlike those during the trip to Yellowstone two years ago) were a combination of meditative satisfaction and thrilling exuberance.

When I returned to Chicago about 9:00 at night I was surprised to find an attractive woman sitting in our living room. She introduced herself as Linda, my roommate Art's cousin, who had come to Chicago and needed a place to stay. Her husband had been grossly mistreating her and she had to get away. I showed her some of my slides of fall color and a number of my creative abstract shots. There was an immediate attraction between us and after talking for several hours we went to bed and made passionate love.

In the morning I learned she had two main job interests: working as a model and reading horoscopes for clients. Her favorite place in Chicago was the art institute. We went downtown together visited the work of our favorite painters and had lunch at the outdoor garden café. It was all very delightful. We stayed together for about a week when Linda decided it was time to move on. She took her daughter (who had been cared for by Art) and headed West with the promise she would write me. She did—a long note about a guy who gave financial seminars on trading commodities all over the country. He hired her mainly to look good in front of his clients. She rented a trailer in the backwoods of Colorado and wanted me to come out and stay with her.

I had no specific plan for the next two months so I took a plane to Denver where she picked me up and we went out to her trailer. She introduced me to her boss and we did some tourist things like going to the Garden of the Gods. Linda had to work during the day when I went exploring with my camera. I told her I felt isolated in the trailer and needed to go back to Chicago to prepare for the next semesters teaching. We agreed to keep in touch.

My second fall semester at St. Xavier College started out fairly well but the year ended in chaos. I began with the same relatively clear mind I had the previous year and my accomplishments were basically acknowledged. There was a change in department chairperson from Stan Boyer to Bob Williams. I never felt close to Bob and had preferred conversing with Stan. My joy of teaching subsided and I looked for a project to work on that would bring me satisfaction. I found it in Kirlian photography. A not exactly scientific approach to taking and interpreting photographs with electricity instead of light.

I built a fairly simple device using an electric transformer that would take 110 Volts from a wall socket and produce 50,000 Volts on a metal plate. For subjects I used mostly leaves. My film was 4x5 color Kodak VPS and the leaves were placed on the film in the dark. Exposing the film with 50,000 Volts produced a truly striking image different in color from the subjects and surrounded by an "aura" of white flashes. I was amazed at how easy it was to make stunning images but I was having difficulty focusing and concentrating even with the excitement of Kirlian photography. My mood had turned lower and I lost the good feelings I had about myself and my work during the last year. Linda had written saying she was moving to Tucson and wanting me to come to visit over Christmas but I lost the enthusiasm I had for her during the summer. I sent her a letter saying I haven't been feeling well recently but if I improve I would meet her in Tucson. Please send a telephone number.

Mapleleaves—"Kirlian" photography

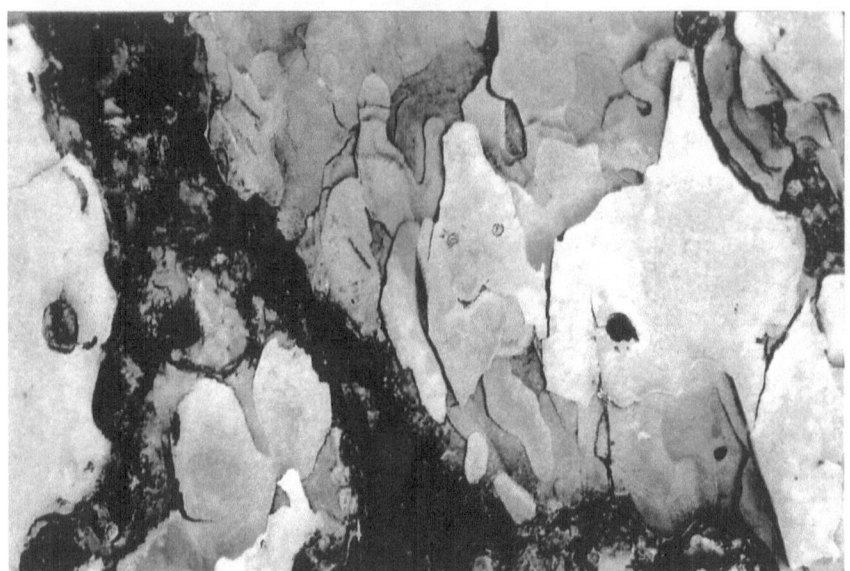

Abstract photo—Staring Profiles—Tree bark up close

In the mean time I met Joanne at a party and we danced romantically. Our eyes met with a longing gaze and we soon got to know each other. She was in the process of getting a divorce and was responsible for two grown male teenagers. Her relationship with her estranged husband had gone very badly the last few years and she found me to be someone she was comfortable with and very attracted to. She had a very good sense of humor and always volunteered to drive me to the airport when I went on a trip. Our relationship began on a relaxed note with mutual caring for each other. Actually before we became romantically involved she served as my realty agent in my attempt to buy a condo.

Condo prices were rising rapidly and everyone thought ownership would be financially sound but I was afraid to follow through on some of the condo units Joanne showed me. I did pursue Joanne romantically and over the next few years we shared a number of romantic adventures. At the same time I became temporarily involved with other women and occasionally became mentally unstable. My friend Jack from the Men's Group had been having problems similar to mine so I asked him if he had gotten any help. He referred me to a psychiatrist at Alexian Brothers Hospital. Dr. Eddington, who had helped him with medication. Dr.

Eddington took notes as I went rapidly through my current complaints. He said I was suffering from "atypical anxiety" and he thought he could help me. I learned later that Dr. Eddington had a national reputation and gave lectures on the treatment of mental illness all over the country. He suggested I take Nardil once a day and 10mg of Valium at bedtime. He explained that I would notice no change in my mood for about one month. At that time he went on to say I would notice a very positive improvement in energy and mood. There were certain foods like aged cheese that I must avoid or I could experience a rapid rise in blood pressure.

A month went by and I continued in my dreary negative outlook. Then within a matter of two or three days I started waking up earlier, about 4:00–5:00am, going into the living room and doing about 50 push-ups and sit-ups and an hour of Yoga. Every day I had a positive outlook and looked forward to my days work. I got a ticket to Florida to visit my parents who had left Harrisburg and who were living in a trailer park in Ft. Lauderdale. My father had bought their first trailer over a year ago when he left his two jobs near Scranton for what reason I never knew. After settling in the trailer park he bought a second trailer either of which could be hitched to the back of his Chevy station wagon. When he heard I was coming to visit he said I could have the second trailer to myself. I looked forward to the visit.

The park supplied water and gas for heating and cooking. For reasons known only to him, my father chose to sleep in the back of his Chevy wagon. My mother was very unhappy with a small kitchen and huge palmetto bugs rushing up and down the walls. At times she would sob quietly to herself. She had had enough of trailer living (it was a small, cheap used unit) and wanted to move into a retirement village. My father was as happy as a lark finding endless activities to get involved in and talking fast and furiously mostly about things known only to himself but when he heard about Linda he blatantly pronounced her a whore and advised me to stay away from her.

Clearly there was no future with Linda and on the spur of the moment I made reservations for a week's vacation at Club Med on Paradise Island. I told Linda I was following my "bliss". She seemed slightly unhappy but said I had to do what I had to do. My father drove me to the airport and within a few hours I was registered in Paradise. It was largely a singles crowd and I was determined to find a suitable woman to sleep with by the end of the week. In the mean time the club had 18 well manicured tennis courts and I played many games. The meals were fabulous, the lunches were buffets with huge mounds of shrimp and the dinners were all you could eat with wine provided as a courtesy, several swimming pools, a show every night and interesting people to meet. The French who owned Club Med were a little stuck up but not a big problem. There was dancing until 2:00am every night.

I don't remember how I met Shirley but the attraction was mutual and we stayed together for the rest of the week, sharing meals, the finals shows, dancing and sleeping together the last night. Making love was different from normal in that I maintained a hard erection for about two to three hours (considerably longer than normal). Shirley invited me to visit her in Worcester, MA during our spring break planning on spending time in Boston. I accepted.

I still had vacation time left when I got back to Ft. Laud and returned to the trailer. My mother was still very unhappy with the living conditions and suggested they take a look at a condo in a retirement village where some of our relatives were living but my father was busy preparing lawsuits against the hospitals where he had been working.

CHAPTER 8
HYPO MANIA

I noticed a distinct change in my mental state. Unusual thoughts came quickly and constantly. Ordinary objects took on strange symbolic appearances. Common objects had a distinct sexual significance and I was convinced that God was in our midst. I suggested to my father that mother had some good ideas about giving up the trailer and moving to a retirement village. But my father was in a stubborn, aggressive hypo-manic mood and was not to be reasoned with. He was enjoying this aberrant way of life pouring energy into future lawsuits that would never prove productive.

I was concerned about my change in mood from a few months ago and finally called Dr. Eddington who offered the suggestion that I was experiencing a "religious conversion" and he gave me the name and author of a book that would explain in more detail. In the mean time he suggested that I cut back on the Nardil. One evening my sister came to visit and Faye, my father, my mother and I took a walk along the Lauderdale Beach. My father talked continuously for several hours about what? I don't remember.

It was time to return to Chicago. Joanna picked me up at the airport. It was the first and last time I visited my parents in the trailer park. Linda called and said she was coming to Chicago with her boss on business. They would stay at the Water Tower Hotel and she suggested I come to visit. When I arrived I found that she was very angry that I never came to Tucson and did not treat me very well. After several hours I left and had a date with Marcy but gave her up to go back to Joanna and prepare for spring semester classes.

Abstract—Sugar crystals—Photomicroscopy

Things were going well at St. Xavier with my classes. I had made over fifty Kirlian photos and arranged for exhibits of my work in the St. Xavier College Gallery and the Chicago Cultural Center in downtown Chicago for the summer. This beautiful building is an icon of culture in Chicago, known for its art exhibits, its beautifully tiled walls and its classical music concerts during lunch hour.

While looking over some science magazines I was attracted to the cover of a magazine that resembled a work of modern art. It was actually a photomicrograph of organic crystals photographed between two polarizing filters (commonly used in sunglasses and on cameras). I began a long term project of making very thin transparent crystals on microscope slides and photographing them through the best microscope I could find in the college which was used by students in the biology classes. The crystals could be made by dissolving substances such as sugar in water and allowing the solution to dry. Another approach is to sprinkle a small amount of a substance such as sulfur on a microscope slide and heat it gently until it liquefies and then allowing it to dry. A 35mm camera body is attached to the monocular viewing tube allowing the view to be seen exactly as it will be recorded on film when the shutter is released. These techniques are really quite common in science laboratories such as Argonne National Laboratories outside of Chicago. It's like a hobby for scientists.

But I hadn't finished with my Kirlian photography project and applied to the International Kirlian Research Association to give a talk in June on the art of Kirlian photography. I was intrigued by the close relationship that I saw between scientific images and the work of modern artists and applied this theme to Kirlian photography. St. Xavier College was kind enough to give me several small project grants to make and exhibit this kind of "art" (science).

In the mean time my "religious conversion" subsided considerably as I weaned myself off Nardil. During our spring vacation I went to visit Shirley in Worcester. When we were in bed together at first she said "I remember the feel of those hands so well." I always felt good when I sensed a woman looked at me in a sensual way. Although the weather was not so good we enjoyed Boston and walked the Freedom Trail which I had never done while in school at MIT. We learned that the old Sigma Alpha Mu fraternity house was changed into a Coed dorm. It was nice being together in a place less frenetic then Club Med was several months ago. Shirley and I went to shows and parties and I invited her to come to Chicago during the summer. She accepted.

During the next few weeks although I acted normally my moods were highly erratic, at times coherent and energetic, at other times incoherent and filled with anxiety. When I returned to Chicago I resumed my teaching routine and continued seeing Joanne. She found me very refreshing after twenty years with a stuffy husband who took her on more camping trips than she cared to go on. When she found he was having an affair she started divorce proceedings. Our social life revolved around folk dances and folk dance activities such as parties and potluck dinners. I had been folk dancing for two years when I was invited to join a folk dance performing group. We rehearsed several times before giving performances at community centers, hospitals, libraries, etc. We dressed in costumes and were generally appreciated by our audience. At the end of the performance we invited members of the audience to join us in simple dances. After the performance we went out drinking, eating and just having fun.

Shirley came to visit in June. We went to shows, parks, parties and walks on the beach. In general I was comfortable having short term relationships with several women at a time. It was usually difficult breaking a relationship. I was living a lifestyle that was not sustainable for me.

My third year at St. Xavier went well. I got a good recommendation from Bob Williams but his last few sentences emphasized although I was performing admirably I needed to concentrate more on the wider life of the university beyond the science department. Somehow I was appointed to the faculty senate. I found the meetings to be very boring, had practically nothing to say and after several months resigned to concentrate on projects in the science department.

I invited Joanne to join me on the trip to New York to give my paper on the art of Kirlian photography. An exceptional thing about the Kirlian photograph of a leaf whose top was cut off was that a second photograph of the leaf revealed an image where the leaf was cut. It was called the "phantom leaf effect" after the human experience of a phantom limb. A New York high school student came to the conference with over 50 pictures of phantom leaves that he had taken. I found them to be remarkable. They seemed to be "genuine". When we first got to New York I felt a sense of anxiety that I couldn't understand. 10mg of Valium served to clear it up. The rest of the time walking through Chinatown, Little Italy, and the Art District were very pleasant and provided good subjects for photographs.

After the conference Joanna took a plane back to Chicago and I went out to Long Island to visit Karen who was studying Biochemistry. She had given up studying dance with Martha Graham sometime ago and was working for a science career. I always regretted that we never established a stronger relationship. She showed me her lab and complained over dinner how it was difficult to meet "suitable" men in her environment.

I returned to Chicago on Friday night. Joanna and I went for a walk along the Lake Michigan shore. Unexpectedly I felt a sense of terror and ran across a field near the beach. After I caught my breath Joanna came up to me to ask what was wrong I said "I didn't know". She asked if I wanted her to stay the night. I said "Yes" and we went back to my apartment. When we had gotten into bed she snuggled up to me wanting to make love. I felt uncomfortable and was not able to sustain an erection. Joanna got angry, got dressed and left. It was about 3:00am and I had trouble sleeping. After several months the effect of Nardil had given me an artificial sense of the soundness of my sexual abilities. In the morning I felt Joanna had left me for good. I was scared and on the verge of "falling apart". I felt I needed to get away and be taken care of. For some reason, I really know not what, I thought spending some time in a mental hospital would be a good idea. I had never spent time in a mental hospital but imagined I would be well taken care of. I called Dr. Eddington who told me he had a bed available in Alexian Brothers Hospital and to come in today. I packed my suitcase and made sure to take my tennis racquet thinking they would have good athletic facilities. How wrong I was.

During the ride to Alexian Brothers Hospital as I went through downtown Chicago I felt the need to pee. Rather than go in my pants I parked illegally and went by the side of a tree. My mind was so distorted I don't know how I got to the hospital. But after parking in the hospital lot I took my suitcase and went to the waiting room. I sat for a while and then played ping pong with a guy who had two racquets and a ball. After a while I wandered down a hallway and came to a door with a small window that I looked through. The sight of severely mentally challenged patients sitting in their pajamas scared the shit out of me. I turned and ran toward the exit but collided with a nurse who I may have knocked down. It seemed like only seconds before I wheelchair was brought up to me. I was put in the chair and strapped down.

The next thing I knew I was in a very small room lying face up on a bed with both arms and legs in tight restraints. The lights in the room were bright and periodically I would hear the screams of a girl, "Let me go!" "Get me the fuck out of here!" Soon I found myself cheering her on. Eventually a nurse and a man came into the room, looked into my eyes and gave me an injection. It was impossible to free myself. So as uncomfortable as I was, I tried to lie still. The nurse and the man came into the room several times. After what seemed like hours of this torture I was released and taken to a bed. So comfortable it seemed I was in heaven.

The next day I found myself in the same room that had scared me and led me to attempt to flee the hospital and I remained in this room several days, sitting and playing with arts and crafts. I made a leather belt. I remember no communication. Eventually I was transferred to a different room where patients talked and were permitted to go for walks around the grounds of the hospital once a day. I met a young woman who I walked with and we talked about many things but I have forgotten the details. I was given medication daily but don't remember being told what it was. At one point Joanna surprised me with a visit. We went for a walk through the halls and found a secluded spot to make love. Was it all a dream?

After about two weeks in the hospital a cat scan was taken of my brain and Dr. Eddington showed me that everything appeared to be normal in my brain. So there was no need to keep me any longer and I was free to leave. No follow up was ever given. As I drove home something seemed strange. My brain did not seem to be normal. I called Joanna and she invited me for dinner. I felt like a little boy and had difficulty comprehending, reading even the simplest of second grade books. Joanna was very kind and would help me with simple tasks. We went to the Evanston Park, watched some puppets and played together. It was about six weeks before St. Xavier classes were to begin but I felt desperately in need of help. I tried an acupuncturist, I tried a chiropractor, I spent time playing Boggle and other games with friends from St. Xavier, anything to get my brain to work again. Joanna drove me to St. Xavier where my labs were incomprehensible to me. I met one of my students who asked if he could do a special project with me. I tried to act as normal as possible and said I would check my schedule.

I was very scared that when fall semester began I would not have recovered well enough to teach. David, who was a psychology teacher, recommended that I see a psychiatrist he knew and trusted, Dr. Robinson. Dr. Robinson was a young man, short and boyish looking. After listening to details of my life over the last year Dr. Robinson suggested I begin taking Nardil as soon as possible. I was given no medication on leaving Alexian Brothers Hospital. There seemed to be something magic about Nardil. No matter how anxious or depressed one was four weeks after taking Nardil one would more than regain his confidence, energy and mental ability.

I returned to the classroom more than ready to teach my classes and interacted appropriately with my new students. Later in the fall I was promoted to associate professor of Physics. I continued to see Dr. Robinson on a regular basis. In an attempt to add humor to my classes I once again gave "awards" to the students who got the two highest grades on tests. The students with the highest grade got a Playboy magazine with a centerfold of a beautiful nature photograph. The student with the second highest grade got a nature magazine with a Playboy centerfold. When the class discovered the true nature of the awards there was considerable laughter. Of course these type of awards were not appropriate in a Catholic School. I simply thought they were clever.

For Christmas vacation I went to Florida to visit my parents and found them living in a retirement condo. It was a two bedroom condo and I had my own bedroom. My father had come down from last year's high and was mildly depressed. I met a psychologist, Wayne, at the local pool. We became friendly and he visited several times. A closer relationship developed between us and he acknowledged he had tried to kill himself several months ago when his wife of thirty years had left him. His intent was to turn on the gas in his oven and put his head inside until he was gone. At the last minute he pulled his head out, packed his suitcase and drove from Baltimore to Florida.

The trailers had been sold and my mother was happy once again. My father did not care for the civilized nature of the village and would have preferred a more natural setting. At the center of the village was a beautiful clubhouse with indoor and outdoor pool, exercise and recreation facilities, meeting rooms, a party room for dances and a 1,200 seat auditorium. As I was leaving a Saturday night dance I saw a woman from a distance and knew almost instantly we'd be in bed together before I went back to Chicago. Ann was a very attractive and sexy woman who was a recently divorced teacher from California. We went snorkeling off the coast, took pictures amongst the Christmas lights in local parks and made plans for a New Year's Eve dinner. Before then we made love on the floor outside her mother's bedroom where Ann felt perfectly at ease. Her mother liked me and thought it would be nice if we got married. After a wonderful New Year's Eve lobster dinner we went dancing and then back to my bedroom to make love. Being with Ann was almost like being in heaven even if we were simply doing our laundry. She invited me to visit her in Long Beach during my school break in January. I got a ticket as soon as possible. We walked on the beach played with her Miniature Collie, went to Disney World, visited my cousin in Palm Beach and made love on her water bed in a candle lit room. While she was teaching I took long bike rides. Before I left California I invited Ann to visit me in Chicago the following month. She looked forward to it and we made plans for the time around Presidents Day.

When I returned to Chicago, Joanna picked me up at the airport and we went back to her place to make love while watching Saturday Night Live. Without thinking what I was saying I told Joanna that I had met Ann in Florida and that she was coming to Chicago to visit me in a few weeks. Understandably she was very hurt and wrote me a poignant letter telling me how much I had meant to her and how much she cared for me. I told Joanna that my fling with Ann was most likely to be short lived and I wanted to continue and expand our relationship.

Ann arrived in Chicago soon after a snow storm but she was well dressed and very cheerful. She visited St. Xavier College, the Chicago Museum of Science and Industry and the Art Institute of Chicago. The weather improved and we took walks along the lake front. She brought me a cake with icing that had an X-rated design. Again she invited me to visit in Long Beach and I accepted.

During my second visit to Long Beach Ann arranged for me to give a workshop on Kirlian photography at Saddleback High School where she taught and I arranged for us to visit Mary Moss, the best known advocate of Kirlian photography in the country. She was a professor of Psychology at UCLA and had been fired for making claims about Kirlian photography that she did not adequately substantiate. The next evening we went to Mary Moss' home and she brought out the Kirlian photos she had taken and I brought a book of Kirlian photos I had taken at St. Xavier. She believed very strongly in the spiritual meaning of her work. Although I was very skeptical of her interpretation I did not criticize her work. She had been fired for a belief that she could not verify. There was sadness in her voice and I told her I was impressed with her courage to claim results that were open to alternate opinions. She liked my work.

The next day I took a Kirlian photo of Ann's dog's paw. A few days before I was to leave it was quite warm but I noticed that a section of her backyard was overgrown with tall weeds. I found a pair of gloves and a hoe in her garage and set about removing the weeds. I worked for several hours and cleared the entire section. When she returned from school Ann looked over the work I had done and said, "You have invaded my space." She went for a walk alone and when she returned she let me know our relationship was not going to work. The warm glow that had filled my body just being near her disappeared. She said she would still like to make love before I left which we did.

I called her several times when I got back from California but eventually she could not be reached. I told Joanna my infatuation was over and we started getting together again. We began by spending the Passover holiday together at a local Jewish Community Center and soon planned a seven day Caribbean cruise for the summer.

We went on the Mardi Gras, my first cruise. There was endless food every hour of the day and up until midnight. We took a tour through the kitchen and saw how the carving of ice statues was done. Most fun was the "night gown contest" for the men. Using Joanna's night gown and make up I entered the contest but did not win the first prize. We stopped at several islands and took tours. I liked the parks and the military fort near San Juan the best. There was relaxing near the pool and dancing after dinner. After making love I got up and went back to dancing until one or two in the morning.

At the end of the summer I resumed my long commute back and forth to St. Xavier. I was taking Nardil on Dr. Robinson's directions on an "as needed basis". While driving back to my apartment one afternoon I became very drowsy. My eyes shut momentarily. After making a turn I ran into a lamp post that was near the road. Fortunately the right side of the car struck the post. If it had been the left side of the car I probably would have been killed. I suffered some minor bruises and a broken bone in my left hand, was taken to a nearby hospital, had my hand bandaged and given a bed to sleep in for the night. I woke up with bad pain in my back and went to a nurse for help. She gave me two Tylenol. I kept complaining about my back pain but I never got more than the two Tylenol. I got no sleep that night. I notified Dr. Robinson of my drowsiness that caused the car accident and he recommended that I change my medication from Nardil to Parnate. The next morning I took the Parnate and was working at my desk when I felt dizzy and nauseous. I called a cab to take me to the hospital but when I threw up slightly in the backseat the driver threw me out of the cab and I walked the last three blocks to the hospital. In the emergency room my blood pressure revealed a hypertensive crisis and I was given an antidote that lowered the pressure. The following day several hours after taking my next dose of Parnate I felt nauseous and dizzy. Once again it was difficult to walk. I called Joanna and asked her if she would take me to the hospital. She replied she would be at my apartment in a few minutes. I was waiting outside when she drove up and I passed out on the way to the hospital. I recovered by the next day but about several hours after taking my dose of Parnate I felt even worse than I did the previous day. I was sure I was seriously ill. I called Joanna once again and after telling her how sick I felt I asked for another ride to the hospital. Again, she said she would pick me up in a short time. Again I was waiting when she pulled up and again I passed out in the car on the way to the hospital. When I woke up I found that I was in the intensive care unit. It was the last time I ever saw Joanna.

A year ago in the fall of 1981, I had literally lost my mind and entered a paranoid state that pushed Joanna to the limit. She had made dinner and tried to comfort me and offered me her love. I had been ranting and raving about a revolution that was going to take place at St. Xavier College. I told her the name of the teacher who was planning on shooting me as I returned home but I spoiled the attempt by taking a different route. I was terribly distraught and not really in touch with reality. Joanna acted as calmly as she could. She invited me to make love and sooth me with inviting words to touch her and hold her in the dark. I fell asleep readily but when I woke up I was once again frantic and raving. Joanna called her good friend Alex to help her deal with me. I was jumping on her bed and started to pee. When Alex arrived they called 911 to send an ambulance to her house.

When the ambulance arrived Alex turned me over to the paramedics who walked with me to the back of the ambulance with its door open. I tried everything I could not to get into the ambulance including crawling underneath the ambulance. Once I was lying down in the bed the ambulance took off. Not knowing where I was going and feeling cold I imagined we were heading North and would eventually get to the North Pole but we stopped at a large building where I was taken to a small room and given some papers to sign. At first I refused but I answered the phone when it rang and was totally surprised to hear the voice of my friend, Sylvia, on the line. She implored me to sign the papers and I would be well taken care of. She warned me that if I refused to sign the papers I would be taken to the state mental institution where I would not be well taken care of. I was fond of Sylvia and trusted her advice so I signed the papers. How she knew where I was remained a mystery to me.

I was taken to a clean private room with a single bed. A doctor and nurse came in and I was told to swallow a pill. I put the pill in my mouth and a minute later spit it out. The doctor then turned me around, pulled down my pants and gave me an injection. I climbed into bed and my mind began racing. I imagined I was in a space craft circling the Earth and could not return from orbit.

Occasionally a doctor would come and ask me some questions. I have no memory of what we talked about, what the meals were like, what the patients in my ward were like, if I was in a ward, how long I stayed in Highland Park Hospital or how I got home but my mind eventually returned to normal.

When I called Joanna I acknowledged that I experienced some kind of mental illness, that I was well taken care of and my mental faculties seemed to have returned to normal. Since I would be considered for tenure in about a year I began to prepare lists, graphs of different types showing the ratings I received from my students, photographs of the new physics lab I installed, the telescopes we used, Kirlian photographs, new courses I introduced, volunteer work I did for the department and the school. It was a big job. The results would be partially used to determine if I were to be granted tenure.

Joanna forgave my horrendous behavior the recent time we were together and we planned a train trip to Seattle for the end of the summer.

Referring ahead to the last time Joanna drove me to the hospital when I woke up I was in intensive care being watched carefully for possible brain damage. When I was removed from intensive care I had two very pleasant surprises. The first was a phone call from my friend, David at St. Xavier College. He was calling to see how I was feeling, to let me know that the teachers at St. Xavier were wishing me a speedy recovery and he was looking forward to our next tennis game. David was my closest friend at St. Xavier and helped me through several difficult times I had with women and school affairs.

The second surprise was to see my father standing by my bedside reassuring me I was in good hands and would soon recover. The doctors decided to do an exploratory operation feeding a tube up through my thigh to the side of my head. They discovered a subarachnoid bleed. Brain surgery was not necessary. I'm not sure if any action was taken or not but I was released from the hospital in about four days. My father was waiting at my apartment when I got home. It was October, the weather was beautiful and the leaves were in full fall color.

My father questioned me about Dr. Robinson, his background and how he was treating me. I got angry and told him that my relationship with Dr. Robinson was personal and private. What a fool I was. My father was trying to help me. I felt guilty for not being more open with him and expressing my thankfulness for coming to Chicago and trying to help me through a serious situation. Several weeks later when my mental faculties were completely normal I went to the library and referred to the PDR (Physician's Desk Reference). Turning to information on Parnate I found at the beginning in large letters, WARNING-wait 10 days before prescribing Parnate to a patient after discontinuing any other MAO (Monoamine Oxidase Inhibitor). I had taken Nardil (a MAO) only a day or two before I took the Parnate that resulted in my ending up in intensive care.

My father left to visit relatives in California and I eventually went back to see Dr. Robinson. His first words were "I suppose you are angry with me." I told him I had referred to the PDR. He said, "We don't take that information very seriously. The PDR is a highly conservative source." I don't recall where my therapy went till months later. At that time the anger I should have had at him back in October surfaced and I attempted to get information on the possibility of suing him by calling several lawyers and getting a copy of my medical records. Every lawyer I called told me the same thing. If I fully recovered from what might be considered mal-practice I have no case against him. I concentrated on completing my records for obtaining tenure.

When I called Joanna she said that she could no longer handle being called upon to take care of my medical needs and never wanted to talk to me again. I tried to show how sorry I was by sending flowers, notes and gifts but I never saw or talked to her again. I was mildly depressed and bought a ticket for Ft. Lauderdale over Christmas vacation to stay with my parents. I invited my father to join me on a bus trip to Tarpon Springs during the Greek New Year celebration. Parades, festivities and dancing, make an interesting getaway. We stopped at Parrot jungle and saw the birds do their tricks. My father met a woman on the bus and spent the whole trip talking with her, laughing and telling jokes. The atmosphere in Tarpon Springs was very festive, the food was great and the dancing was exuberant. The trip was especially memorable because it was the last time I ever saw my father.

Upon returning to Chicago my mood got worse. Even though my seventy page report on success with all my classes as well as the projects I worked on and volunteering to take part in college activities I was anxious about my chances of getting tenure mainly because of the newest chairperson of the science department—Sister Eleanor. She did not care for my liberal style of teaching and several times criticized my class work that she observed. She was highly conservative and our philosophies of teaching did not mesh. As my behavior deteriorated I began to think of going into the hospital once again. This was a very bad mistake but my confidence level was at a low ebb even though several colleagues from the history department stopped by my office and urged me to stand up for my record. I called Dr. Robinson (another bad mistake) and asked his advice. He told me to come into the hospital where I would be well treated and come out with confidence intact.

I was in a terrible ambivalent state but packed a suitcase and asked one of my roommates to drive me to the hospital. The next thing I knew I was in a bed with restraints on my arms and ankles. Dr. Robinson came to visit. He said he had never seen anyone as depressed as I was and was sorry to tell me that my father had died two days ago from a massive heart attack. He was found alone in the retirement village sauna lying on the top bench. I was speechless and very sad. My mother handled all the funeral arrangements which included a casket burial in the ground contrary to my father's wishes for a cremation. For years to come when

I came to the retirement village to visit my mother and sister I enjoyed using this sauna. Inevitably a man would bring up a warning not to stay in the sauna alone "A man, he was a doctor, fell asleep on the top shelf and died." I usually responded, "Yes, it was my father and he loved saunas." I recovered from my anxiety and depression rather quickly but was kept in the locked ward for more than a month. There were games to play, backgammon being one of my favorites, and we were permitted to take a walk from the hospital to the Lake Michigan lakefront once a day accompanied by a male nurse. I begged to be released but resorted to playing games with the nurses, going on trips to a nearby bowling alley and taking daily walks.

I was finally released sometime in late March and made an appointment with the academic dean who would determine my fate at St. Xavier. The dean was a fair and pleasant man. He asked about my health and offered to write me a letter of recommendation to any college to which I may be applying. However after three hospitalizations in one year I hadn't shown the stability that St. Xavier requires of its teachers and he offered me three choices: Resign from the school, take a one year sabbatical at half pay or admit I had a long term illness and get one year's full pay before resigning.

I didn't want the illness on my record so I took the one year sabbatical which I would use to upgrade the two semester astronomy course I had been teaching. In the mean time I looked for both full-time and part-time teaching positions. I was able to find three part-time positions. One at Oakton Community College in Physics, one at Triton Community College in Astronomy and one at Columbia College in Optics and Holography.

While I was in the hospital I got a call from Dr. Porth, a psychologist who said he could help me and to call him when I got out of the hospital. I had always seen myself as a college teacher but I began to consider high school teaching. I accepted teaching one course at Oakton Community College in the fall but also enrolled in a summer course at Northeastern University to begin working towards getting a high school teaching certificate. I hated the Northeastern course and considered it a total waste of time. I mistakenly decided to discontinue taking teacher training courses at Northeastern and continued with part-time teaching.

This was a mistake but I simply wasn't thinking clearly. I obsessed with the events of the last year and the fact that my father had died.

During the last summer I had a one man exhibit of my Kirlian photography at a local library. I was surprised to get a phone call from a neighbor, Joe, who had seen the exhibit, was impressed by it and wanted to find out more details. He invited me to his apartment, introduced his wife and we became friends. During the late fall I slowly became more dysfunctional as a teacher and felt like I was entering a bad dream.

I met an interesting woman, Katherine, at a singles dance and as we got into bed she told me she had a breast removed due to cancer. I said I was not upset by her revelation and we made very pleasant love but I was too distraught to keep calling her.

One of the men who was in our original men's group had become an Orthodox Jew. I called him for advice on proper mourning for a parent and he invited me to his home for Friday night dinner. It was the middle of December and dark by 5:30pm with light snow falling. I tried to follow the directions to his home. I went south past Touhy Avenue and went past Touhy Avenue again about five blocks later. I felt like I was entering the twilight zone and became very frightened. I turned the car around went north and past Touhy Avenue once again. At this point I was in a state of panic, left my car in the middle of the road and started walking toward my apartment. Several buildings looked familiar. I saw a Synagogue across the street and considered going inside, down to the basement and crying my eyes out. Then an old age home appeared in front of me. I climbed the half flight of steps, went inside and saw a very elderly lady sitting in a wheelchair. I went up to her and began kissing her on the forehead. Then I saw another elderly lady in a wheelchair and went up to her and began kissing her on the cheek. You could say I had gone out of my mind or entered a bad dream.

As I turned around I saw two policemen who came up to me and escorted me into an empty police patty wagon. It was dark and cold and I had no idea where I was. We made several stops and I was asked to show my ID. It seemed as if we had traveled at least an hour before we stopped and I entered a room where I sat for a while before some paperwork was done and I was given a pair of pajamas and taken to a small room empty except for a bed.

Eventually it dawned on me that I had been placed in the Read Zone State Mental Facility. I have little memory of how I spent my time there. I was given medication. I did have visitors. Katherine brought me homemade banana bread and wished me a speedy recovery. Nancy also came by with good wishes for a speedy recovery. I was released in about two weeks. Nancy came and drove me home.

I had met Nancy at a dance and we went out a few times before I disappeared into the state mental facility. I called her a few days after I was released from the hospital. She invited me to visit her and seduced me fifteen minutes after I entered her apartment. I felt very awkward since I had not fully recovered from my stay at Reed Zone. The next day she took me to a rehab center where she worked and I heard a lot of women screaming.

I had no job and developed a routine of going to the library and reading magazines and newspapers all morning. In the afternoon I would work out and try to return to the real world. I saw Nancy twice a week but she was very jealous. Even my talking about other women threw her into a tantrum. She was a good person but our backgrounds were totally different and we drifted apart.

During the summer I did a lot of bike riding, photography, dancing and meeting friends at the beach on weekends. I put together a good portfolio of my unique photography and took it to some of the better known galleries in Chicago. A few of them showed interest in my work.

I met Jayne at a Sunday night singles dance in early October. Although she was eleven years older than me she was very attractive with a great figure and she wore unique outfits based in American Indian styles. She was a Ph.D. Psychologist who worked out of her home but had many other interests including running a small quiet resort in western Illinois and taking trips to Columbia, South America where she bought Alpaca and had a local seamstress turn the material into exotic sweaters which she sold here in America. She also was an amateur sculptor.

After the dance I walked her to her car and invited her to follow me home. She proposed that I come over to her home the next Wednesday. I accepted. She showed me a catalogue of the Alpaca sweaters she designed, some of her sculptures and some of the paintings her son had given her. She was the first Ph.D. I had an interest in since Janet, my ex wife. Making love with her was a real pleasure. The next time we got together she invited me to spend a weekend with her at her resort. I had made plans to spend the weekend at a singles event in Wisconsin. She wanted me to break my plans and we got into a real argument which annoyed me but we settled for going out to western Illinois the following weekend. We spent most of the time in bed again with great pleasure.

I had been planning a large party for the next weekend for my friends and students at St. Xavier, tennis players and especially folk dancers. I asked Jayne to come and she arrived in one of her Indian outfits with exotic feathers. Although we had a few minor arguments in the next few weeks she suggested we get an apartment downtown and live together. I thought to myself this was not a good idea at all for several reasons. I could not afford it, we had gotten into several squabbles that lasted far too long where she played a dominant role and was not adept at compromising. She was really too old for me. The party was really great with good food and drinks, a lot of dancing, music, singing and students smoking pot on the back porch. During the next week Jayne and I went to an expensive exhibit of the Impressionists at the art Institute. I noticed that the expansive mood I had been in over the last few months began to falter. I felt no enjoyment of the art works which I normally found very appealing. I didn't know how to handle Jayne's offer to live together. I should simply have said no. I lost my concentration and enjoyment of everyday events but things got much worse rather quickly. I had accepted the responsibility of teaching courses at three different colleges. My first class at Columbia College was in downtown Chicago in the morning.

As I drove south on the outer drive I looked across Lincoln Park and saw the buildings were crumbling. I was scared that downtown Chicago would fall apart. I turned around and headed north to Dr. Porth's office. As I approached his office I felt he could offer no help so I turned into the Skokie Lagoons and slowly returned to my apartment. On the way back I saw a repairman making some connections at the top of what looked like a telephone pole. I was afraid he was preparing to hang me and I drove faster.

The snow on the trees was especially beautiful and I took my camera out of the car and took several pictures. I forgot about my other classes and went home.

My best friend from high school, Jerry, was living in Cincinnati and was a practicing psychiatrist. I gave him a call and tried to describe my distraught mental condition. He offered to drive up to Chicago that night to talk. He arrived after midnight and could see that I was talking too much and too fast and not making much sense. He suggested I get on Lithium right away.

In the morning Jerry, Jayne and I got together for breakfast. Jerry and Jayne concluded that I needed professional help but could do nothing if I refused to get on Lithium. Ever since I started seeing Dr. Porth he strongly urged me to get off Lithium saying it was a crutch and I needed his therapy.

He suggested I was a wimp and addicted to something that took away my genuine feelings and ability to deal with them. After pushing me for several months I had stopped taking Lithium. Jerry was a true friend and gave up his weekend to explain that my severe mental distortions were chemical in nature and that a return to Lithium would make it possible to think rationally but I was too confused. I was convinced that Dr. Robinson was not confident to handle my severe mood changes. I had gone downhill rapidly and was suffering from severe delusions. I was totally irresponsible and after a few attempts to get to my classes I began taking alternate routes to avoid what I imagined was the gradual degradation of the city. I never reported my problems to any of the three department chairmen where I was teaching.

I couldn't trust anybody and stopped leaving my apartment. One of my roommates had a cat that would scratch the bottom of my bedroom door. I woke up and imagined that the cat was a fierce tiger that was trying to mangle me. Finally, I called my friend Jack and asked him to drive me to my doctor (internist). I didn't think about how I would get home. As we pulled into the parking lot of the large building where the doctor had her office I saw one window was open and may have been broken. I imagined someone was going to throw me out of the window. I thanked Jack and went into the waiting room. I didn't know where I was and I didn't recognize "my doctor". She asked me to sit down and I refused. I was completely uncooperative and didn't follow any of her instructions. I didn't even know who she was. Finally she asked me to sit in the waiting room. In about ten minutes two policemen entered the room and withdrew their guns. They asked me to come with them or they would carry me away. A wagon was waiting down stairs and for the second time I was thrown into the back of an empty paddy wagon. I was truly in the depths of hell.

I was taken to Read Zone State Mental Health Center for the second time. This time I remembered much more. After filling out paperwork two guards picked me up and carried me to a bed in a small room where two other men were sleeping.

The man in the middle bed would wake up every so often, pound on his bed and scream obscenities. He threatened to kill people I didn't know. I huddled under my blanket and prayed I would survive the night.

In the morning I awoke and went out into a large room with an old TV set and picture windows with frost on part of them and a view of an open field covered with snow. There were about eight to ten people of different ages wandering around the room or watching TV. One woman in a night gown was lying on the floor urinating. Another woman held her arms out in front of her and walked back and forth. It was said that when she was released she would walk down to one of the beaches of Lake Michigan and start walking into the lake. When she was rescued she was taken back to Read Zone. Around noon we formed a line and were given our medication. I didn't know what I was given but I took it.

My mental state varied from relative clarity to muddled confusion. After several days I was given an appointment with a man who I thought was a psychologist. He asked me some questions but had a bad cold and was constantly sniffling and blowing his nose. I recognized the head doctor in the ward and when my head was clear I would plead to be released. "In due time." he said "In due time". Unexpectedly a cheerful Joe Lindstrom, my neighbor, came to visit and brought a bag of fruit. He said he was glad to see me and would drive me home when I was released. Gradually my head cleared and I was released with a prescription for Tofranil (I believe). I got a ticket for Ft. Lauderdale as soon as I could to visit my mother.

My father had always handled the financial affairs of the family. All his assets were left to my mother. I was concerned because she could barely balance a check book. Again I was wrong. She handled my father's investments (mostly in corporate bonds) very well and tripled her assets in fifteen years. She also had her condo completely remodeled. I was surprised at how capable she was when given the chance to make her own decisions.

Since she had always allowed my father to take charge and make family decisions I also assumed she would live the rest of her life without male companionship. Again I was wrong. A year later she met a man in the synagogue and they developed a very close friendship. Al had a great sense of humor and came from a good family that looked after him. She made him nice dinners and they went to hotels on Miami Beach for the weekend. I spent most of my vacation time recovering from the trauma of the time I spent in the Read Zone.

When I returned to Chicago I established a routine of going to the Evanston Library every morning and reading the newspapers and monthly magazines. My part time teaching jobs disappeared of course and I spent the second semester in a variety of activities. By studying the closing prices of corporate bonds in the Wall Street Journal I came to the conclusion that while bond prices may temporarily fall, they almost always recovered their value. Many of the so called junk bonds were paying 20-30% interest at this time. I had bought a number of these bonds several years ago and made a very reasonable profit. I started buying junk bonds this time convinced I would, once again, make a tidy profit.

Trying to get a full time college teaching job, was so frustrating that I worked as a photographic assistant. I started seeing Jayne and we were getting along well together. We went cross-country skiing along the lakefront and had wonderful walks in the snow-covered forest reserves. I did more photography for her sweater business. We went together for a weekend to her resort.

I got friendly with Mary who I met at a party. She lived right on the lakefront and we began running a few miles up and down the lakefront early every morning. She had previously dated one of my roommates, Andy, until she claimed he cheated her out of $5,000 in a financial deal. She invited me for dinner one Saturday night with flowers, incense, wine, and lovemaking, but I politely declined the lovemaking. I needed friends, not more lovers at this point.

In order to get more training as a photographer, I took lessons from a well-known professional portrait photographer in Skokie. The amount of professional equipment required was substantial. To bring more money in, I worked for a photographer as a black and white printer at which I had considerable experience. My junk bond plan was not working well causing some anxiety.

When I saw a notice of a meeting of the Manic Depressive Society at a local restaurant once a month I attended out of curiosity and hoped that I might find some members from whom I could get some guidance. I had a lengthy conversation with the president of the group, Dawn Sugarman. We struck up a conversation and became friendly. When I was feeling lost, she invited me to start making hospital visits to society members who were having a particularly hard time.

The power of the illness struck me not only in my own family, but in listening to stories of friends from folk dancing circles. My friend and good tennis player, Melody, told me about her former husband, David, who was the youngest full professor of mechanical engineering at I.I.T. (Illinois Institute of Technology) when he was 35 years old. They had two lovely children and lived in a fashionable suburb north of Chicago. David became depressed to the point that he was hospitalized. The former details of his mental condition I do not know, but Janet said that he was able to get hold of a large supply of Valium, took all the pills at once and was found dead in his bed. Raising her children by herself was very difficult to say the least, but she had a very positive attitude and got professional help. She also had a boyfriend who lived downtown and had frequent parties to which he invited professional musicians and artists. His apartment was like a museum and I was pleased to be an invited guest.

Another woman I become friendly with was somewhat older, a very good dancer, and frequent teacher of new folk dances. She would use folk dancing as a means of getting away from her husband who she claimed was a "rapid cycler" manic depressive. One day she had come home to find her husband had bought a horse and left it in the backyard.

After spending some time with Dawn I invited her and her boyfriend, Henry, for dinner. Henry was very bright and had a good job working for a chemical company. He spoke in a very authoritative manner practically nonstop. Dawn was divorced from a very wealthy man and got a good financial settlement. She devoted a large part of her time to managing the Manic Depressive Society and offering personal support to members of the Society who were having special difficulties.

One evening she called me sounding quite distressed and asked if she could come over to my apartment for a while. Of course I said yes. I was surprised to see her in such an anxious state. She wasted no time in telling me that her friend Henry had killed himself. I was shocked, but not nearly as much as Dawn. I asked her to sit down and offered her a drink. She did not seem to want to discuss details and asked if she could take a shower. I said yes and got her a towel. After her shower, she said she was tired and could we get into bed together. I wanted to be helpful, but was concerned where this situation was leading. I never had any sexual feelings for Dawn and when she said will you make love with me I politely said no. She was furious, got dressed and left without saying goodbye.

In the meantime, I continued seeing Jayne. Once again she planned a trip with me over Memorial Day weekend to her resort. To prepare for the trip she asked me to carry some books from her second floor apartment down to the steps leading into her building. Unaware of the precision of her request I placed the books up against the wall of her building. When she saw what I had done she screamed at me for not following her simple directions: "On the steps!" she screamed. She couldn't seem to get rid of her anger and demanded an apology from me or she would not take me to the resort for the weekend. I had no other plans and apologized, hoping she would resume her more or less pleasant demeanor.

She had some plans for doing some work around the resort grounds and I offered to help wherever I could, but it seemed that whatever I did was contrary to her plans and her anger would flare up at me. At one point she ran away and when she returned she said, "Get in the car. I'm taking you to the train station. You can get a train back to Chicago." Considering her constant angry mood I should have gotten away from her as quickly as possible. Yet I remember thinking on the train of ways that I could clear matters up. When I got to my car I had written a note telling her how much I cared for her and wanted to get together again. I taped the note to her car's window.

A few days later I got a note from Jayne telling me how "colorful" she thought I was and that she would like to get together. If most psychologists had Jayne's temperament I pity their poor patients. In any case we made plans for spending the 4th of July at Zion Park—a quiet beach forty miles North of Chicago. We brought bicycles and a tent as well as a nice lunch. After lunch we set up the tent and made love inside for most of the afternoon. She was a very good lover which seemed to make up for her fits of anger. We took a slow route back to Chicago and stopped to watch a fantastic lightning display over Lake Michigan. She brought me some tomatoes from her garden and said Goodbye in September.

I had no steady work the entire year. Since I needed income I got several part-time jobs over the next few years. The first job I accepted was an Assistant Photographer for Krantzden and Company (the largest tabletop photography company in the country). Their accounts included Sears and Montgomery Ward. They occupied all 11 floors of a building that covered one square block. They used 8" by 10" view cameras and photographed objects as small as jewelry and as large as an entire room of furniture. I hated the job. I loved shooting nature scenes and abstract work. Commercial work was very unpleasant to me and I guess I must have made my feelings known to my boss. He fired me after three months.

A few weeks later I got a job as an Assistant with a local photographer who specialized in shooting onsite photography. My responsibility was largely in setting up the lighting and wiring and carrying the equipment to the appropriate position. Needless to say I was very unhappy with this job also but stayed on for several months. I stayed over Christmas and New Years, the first time I did not go to Florida in years.

During the last half year I met regularly with a counselor at Jewish Vocational Service who had a list of low paying jobs. Mrs. Wolfson was a delightful woman who could cheer me up with her wit and humor. We had friendly, personal conversations and she even found me a job working in a camera store. The store had been run by a somewhat elderly couple for over forty years. I sold camera equipment, took orders for prints, gave advice on camera equipment and took passport photos. We accepted only cash for passport photos—no income tax due. I would begin my day by running with Mary, work 9-5 and spend most of the night in front of the TV. Two nights a week I taught Physics once again at Oakton Community College. It was a dreary existence but I was only mildly depressed.

One spring morning as I was driving to Oakton in foggy weather, I dozed off and hit the car in front of me. My face hit the windshield and my upper lip was sliced in half. I was taken to a local hospital and a nearby plastic surgeon was called in. My face was swollen for several weeks but the surgeon did a fantastic job sewing me up without any trace of an injury. One of the women in my class invited me for dinner with her husband. Sandy was a darling, looked a lot like Goldie Hawn and was one of the brightest students in my class. She sat in the front row and would look up at me and bat her eyelashes. After the class was over I asked her to come visit at my apartment, but she insisted I go to her apartment which I did. She had a large wooly dog which she insisted stay in the bedroom with us. The dog seemed curious as to what was happening in the bed. Sandy was not a very good lover. She remained almost perfectly still while I did all the work. We got out of bed, got dressed and were sitting in the living room when unexpectedly her husband came home from work early. I left the apartment as fast as I could but not before he threatened to kill me if I ever came back to see Sandy. Sandy was not well and was put into a local hospital a few weeks later. I brought her a bunch of flowers but did not continue to visit her.

I continued my dreary routine of working at the camera store and watching TV. Because I didn't feel good about myself I went to only one dance a week, a folk dance and refrained from socializing with a lot of people I had been very friendly with. I often lay in bed fantasizing that I would never have a normal life again and would die a pauper but I continued running with Mary and joined a Sunday afternoon walking club but had little to say.

CHAPTER 9

FINDING ORIENTATION

One day as we were running back to Mary's apartment I was overwhelmed with feelings of hopelessness and didn't say a word. Mary said "Jerry, why don't you get that teaching certificate and teach high school. You know the salary would be better than college teaching and you would be respected." Although I had discounted high school teaching in the past, this time Mary's words made sense to me and helped to save my life.

I reenrolled in the Northeastern University Teaching Certificate Program and began in September by taking three courses. It infuriated me to know that if Albert Einstein wanted to teach high school in Chicago he would have to take the same nine courses that I needed. As I was enrolling, a secretary asked me what courses I had taken so far. I told her to go fuck herself. A few days later my advisor talked to me personally and suggested I see the University's Counselor, Mr. James. Mr. James told me that he knew exactly how I felt but it was expected that I follow the school rules regardless of how I felt. There were three other Ph.D.'s in my class who were resigned to take the same courses that I was. Using bad language and insulting school personnel would not help my cause. After my first meeting with Mr. James I continued to see him on a regular basis, to express my feelings to a person who was empathetic and understood my situation. He was very helpful in listening when I had anger to vent at the "system".

I did a good job in all of my classes and actually liked Dr. Stoltz's class in Science Teaching Methods. We were required to prepare and give a sample lesson in our field, in my case—Physics. I prepared an inclined plane and several different sized balls and cylinders which we timed as they rolled down the plane. Which ball would get to the bottom first? I gave prizes to the students who guessed the correct answer. I titled the lesson "Why are Physics teachers still playing with their balls?"

After the next class Dr. Stoltz took me aside and explained that several women in the class told him they were offended by my sexual reference. I told him I understood some of their feelings and would try to refrain from using sexual innuendoes in class. Teaching was beginning to feel like fun again.

For the last six weeks of the course we were assigned to a high school for practice teaching. I was assigned to Glenview North, one of the North Shore's most well equipped and highest ranked schools. I had two excellent supervisors, Elane Bloom and Roger Smith. Elane was highly versed in the details of our space program and on the list for astronaut training. Roger taught the advanced physics course with calculus. Half of his students went on to Ivy League schools. There was a problem with some of the students who came from families with incomes 5-10 times that of the teachers. They felt the teachers were there to serve them and even to take instructions from them.

I taught two regular classes and an AP class and did creative things like presenting a slide show of pictures of Einstein showing the personal side of the man. At one point that little devil arouse in me and I once again gave prizes to students who got the best test grades—a Playboy Magazine with a Nature centerfold to the student with the best grades and a Nature magazine with a Playboy centerfold to the student with the second highest grades. At the end of the day my supervisor informed me that the science department chairman wanted to see me the first thing in the morning. My heart beat increased as well as my blood pressure as I realized I had jeopardized the good job I had been doing and may even have failed the student teaching course. I rehearsed my response to Dr. Mittleman, filled with apologies for my inappropriate method of rewarding High School students for their good grades. Dr. Mittleman emphasized that my behavior was totally lacking in good judgment but accepted my apology and gave me a good recommendation for the work I had done in student teaching.

One beautiful spring afternoon I was visiting Carol and told her I was going to strip to my underwear and take a walk around the neighborhood. She remarked that I was not using good judgment and perhaps I should get some professional help. I made an appointment with Mrs. Wolfson at JVS who recommended that I call a psychiatrist whom she praised highly. After listening to my stories of depressive periods beginning at age 28 that played havoc with my attempt to lead a satisfying life the psychiatrist, Dr. Conroe, suggested that I take Lithium on a regular basis. My first manic episode took place two months after taking Nardil when I was 35. Lithium had been prescribed for me prior to seeing Dr. Conroe but I did not take it on a consistent basis. It did not have any side effects for me and I had no good reason not to take it regularly. Dr. Conroe had me take a Lithium level test every three months to check that the Lithium was in a normal blood level. I saw Dr. Conroe on a steady basis and he provided a background that kept my moods at a fairly normal level. After experience with several psychiatrists and psychologists who had either misdiagnosed or mistreated me, I had a doctor in whom I could trust.

We graduated in early June and with my high school teaching certificate in hand I quickly set about looking for a permanent job. An opening was available for a Physics teacher in a nearby Catholic high school. It had a good reputation and I liked the principal very much. They had good lab equipment and were very happy to offer me the position. The salary was low but teaching conditions were excellent. I signed a contract.

Two weeks later I heard about an opening in a south suburban high school for a Physics teacher to teach two regular classes, an honors class and an AP class. Although it was an hour's commute I went for an interview with Mrs. Stillman. Mrs. Stillman was in charge of Academic Programs and was impressed with my background. She offered me the position at a salary considerably higher than that at the Catholic school.

I knew a few of the teachers at Lincoln High school and asked them a number of questions regarding teaching conditions at the school. The student body was basically ninety percent black and students entered the high school with poor academic backgrounds but on the whole they were cooperative, appreciated the opportunity for extracurricular activities and a reasonable percentage of the students went on to college.

Since the difference in salary was significant and I could use the money since I hadn't had a full time job in six years I went back to the President of the Catholic school, Sister Sarah, and told her my situation in a very straightforward way. I really liked the atmosphere at the Catholic school but my financial situation made Lincoln High School very attractive and I politely asked to cancel my contract. I got permission and spent some time over the summer getting my classroom and laboratory in good condition. I had a budget for Physics equipment which I used to purchase new experiments. There was a store room between the Physics class and a Biology class. Hank, the Biology teacher, was not very neat in storing his equipment and I took the time to organize the store room.

Around the 4th of July, Carol and I planned a camping trip to Door County with her friends, which was very pleasant. We went biking and had some good cookouts. Carol liked outdoor activities. She was also a talented singer. I was usually attracted to women who had interests different from mine.

The following spring I was invited to a roller skating party to raise money for charity. I was a good ice skater but had no experience roller skating. I accepted the invitation and began skating slowly and cautiously to get the feel of the skates.

It was a pleasant sensation and I gradually began to pick up speed. Soon I was experiencing a feeling of exhilaration but there was a problem, I did not know how to stop, eventually lost my balance and found myself on the floor with my legs spread out underneath me in terrible pain. A friend helped me off the floor since I could stand on my own feet. My friend also helped me to a local hospital where X-Rays showed I had no broken bones. My knees were bandaged and I was given a pair of crutches and released. The doctor told me I had a torn anterior cruciate ligament (ACL) which would not heal on its own. Arthroscopic surgery would help temporarily but I would probably need surgery in 10 to 20 years.

Carol and I planned a rafting trip on the Green River which runs into the Colorado River. Overall, it is fairly smooth but there are several rapids. My knee was bandaged at the time we left for the trip but I could walk fairly well and even did some hiking along the way. I really liked the experience of rafting a river like the Green. The scenery consists of high multicolored cliffs with interesting geologic formations. The stillness in the air became apparent after a while and the sensation of being carried past continually changing scenery is delightful. There were eight passengers and two professional oarsmen who made us feel we were in competent hands. We never saw another person during the entire length of the six day trip.

CHAPTER 10

TEACHING HIGH SCHOOL

The second year at Lincoln High saw a slight change in my teaching schedule. There were not sufficient qualified students for an AP Physics class so I had three regular classes and two honors classes. From the previous year I had learned how important discipline was. When the students were in the room I spoke in a loud voice "When the bell rings you should be in your seats with your mouths shut." At first the students kept talking for a while, but when I started handing out detention slips the talking quickly stopped. This was a class of honors students and they had good study habits but were used to a more laid back atmosphere. When one of the best students in the class told his mother that the Physics teacher shouted at them I got a phone call from his mother complaining that I was being too harsh with the class. I replied that I was aware David was a very good student but we could cover more material if there was more order in the class. Eventually a good relationship was established between me and the students.

In addition to teaching five courses a week with labs I served as the ACT science reasoning Prep Tutor, the Mathletes Judge and Field Trip Organizer and Coordinator. I worked well with our department chair, Janie, and volunteered to show off the physics and astronomy courses to parents on an open house day. I taught additional college courses in Astronomy at Prairie State Junior College and assisted students with art projects in Kirlian photography at Columbia College.

In early Spring I had an offer from the People to People Youth Science Exchange Program to lead a group of twenty-five highly motivated high school students from all over the country to Russia to meet with a group of twenty-five Russian students in the small village of Bukova, site of the world's largest telescope at the time. In the mornings we had lectures by local Astronomers and on some afternoons we would go by bus up the nearby mountain where the telescope was located and learned how it worked. We were the first group of Americans to visit Bukova and were welcomed graciously. Social activities were planned for some afternoons and evenings. The students got along very well together. One of the purposes of the program was to build openness and friendship between the students of the two countries. It was 1990 and we were still in the Soviet Union.

In addition to the academic program which lasted about three weeks we also toured Moscow, St. Petersburg and Russia's finest ski resort in the beautiful Caucasus Mountains. An optional hiking and camping trip was available up into the twin peaks area, with truly beautiful scenery. Some of the highlights of our touring included St. Basil's Cathedral, the Kremlin with all its gold covered domes, the large department store, GUM, Moscow University and the incredibly clean subway system. A trip by hydroplane out to the summer home of Saint Peter the Great, which had been completely destroyed during WWII and was totally rebuilt after the war, the Hermitage, one of the largest museums or art in the world and a ballet performance by one of the touring companies of the Bolshoi Ballet. The opportunity to see so much of Russia was fantastic.

The chance to meet and talk with the parents of some of the Russian students was very enjoyable. The emphasis on sharing our ways of life was very satisfying. We felt a closeness with the Russian people which continued for several years of writing letters.

Russian Orthodox Churches—The Kremlin

From the very beginning of our adventure in Russia we had a guide who spoke perfect English. Katrina was a student majoring in Economics at the University of Moscow. She was very helpful in arranging our transfers from one place to another and very knowledgeable about Russian history and customs. She made our trip very comfortable and we couldn't have had a better guide in our Russian travels. She decided to come to the University of Chicago for Grad school in Economics and we had a chance to have lunch together.

In the spring before we left for Russia I had met an elegant, graceful woman at the Evanson Folk Dance Group. Paula and I went dancing in downtown Chicago and a mutual attraction between us developed rapidly. Before leaving for Russia I invited her to join me on a fourteen day folk dancing cruise to Alaska. Fantastic scenery, folk dancing on the deck and walking through Alaskan towns made a wonderful vacation.

When Carol heard I was going to Alaska a week after returning from Russia she was understandably upset. There was little time planned for us to be together. My preference was to be with Paula.

I'm glad I went to Alaska in 1990. Except for Juneau, the capital of Alaska, the seaside towns were colorful and rustic and the people had a definite look of independence. Each town had its own character and walking from one end to the other was easy. The moss covered cabins gave a clue that the annual rain fall was about 140" a year.

Mendenhall Glacier—20 miles North of Juneau

I took a second cruise to Alaska in 2003. The changes were extreme. The towns were saturated with tourists walking up and down the main streets carrying their bags of souvenirs. The stores and restaurants had become upscale.

Being with Paula was very pleasant. She chose to spend a good part of our time taking dance lessons from our Turkish teacher. I wanted to spend as much romantic time with her as I could.

Upon returning from Alaska, I called Carol and wanted to see her. When I first came to her apartment it was clear she was very unhappy with me. She demanded to know if I met any women on the cruise and I said no and tried to change the subject to the magnificent scenery and incredible glaciers. We made love in an attempt to smooth things over. Being involved with two women at the same time was never easy but something I did quite frequently.

The next night I had a date with Paula. It was only two days since I had seen her. She too had become jealous and wanted to know if I had seen Carol the day before. My tendency had usually been to be straight forward with these questions. I said "Yes, I did." Paula became furious and said she did not want to see me again. This only made me more desirous to see her. I called, we talked, she said she would think it over and let me know in a few weeks. How thrilled I was when she said she still wanted to see me. Her wonderful smile when we met was exciting and making love was just as great as it was a few weeks ago. Sunday afternoon before I left she gave me a Feldenkries treatment. She was studying to be a Feldenkries Therapist. I felt great and was surprised to get a call from her two days later saying she wanted to come over to talk with me. She got right to the point and said she decided she did not want to see me anymore. She had found her "bliss", a term used by Joseph Campbell, in the form of a short 75 year old balding man she met folk dancing. I was furious and we went for a walk and talked for over an hour. When she got home I called and we talked until the sun came up. I got up, showered, ate breakfast and got to school before 7:30am. It was difficult to focus on the lessons. I went back to Carol and we started dating again. Certainly my behavior was inconsistent. It took some time to straighten things out. Overall it was an adventurous summer.

Returning to Lincoln H.S. seemed fairly routine. But during my first visit with Mrs. Stillman she suggested that I apply for a Presidential Award—for the best high school teacher in Illinois. Even though there were gaps in my background she felt my overall record was exemplary. I got to work and filled out an application as completely as I could. Mrs. Stillman then volunteered to edit and embellish it. She had been an English major and was a good writer. When she was finished with the application it was highly polished and I submitted it.

About this time I was fascinated with a scientific magazine that had a cover filled with an intricate pattern of magnified colorful crystals. I learned that such photos could be created using two polarizing filters, a microscope and micro crystals deposited on a microscope slide. I borrowed a microscope from the Biology department, bought the filters from American Science Center and made the crystals myself. This technique has been used for many years in forensic work. I became fascinated by the photos I made of crystals that had a strong resemblance to works of modern art.

I received several small project grants from the school and put together an exhibit of the crystal photos and prepared a presentation on the subject "Is it Science or is it Art?" which I gave at meetings in the Chicago area such as Illinois Math and Science Academy, Illinois Science Teachers Association and American Association of Physics Teachers. At times I got carried away and worked on my photos till after midnight.

At the same time I began to look for another girlfriend. By coincidence Mary was working for Larry Landon in the same room as Molly, whom she recommended that I call. We met at a pizza parlor and found mutual attraction. Molly was an artist who worked for a travel organization that planned trips to art centers all over the world. She also loved singing in a local choir of 120 people (we had a mutual interest in travel and planned trips to over twenty national parks in the US and 15 countries all over the world. At first they were mostly camping trips, then we switched to bed and breakfast trips and finally to cruises.)

In our discussion over pizza I found that Molly was in the process of a divorce and after a period of depression, went to Israel where she served as a volunteer in the Israeli Army. There she met Dick with whom she spent some vacation time and later accepted an invitation from him to spend some time in Guatemala. She had just returned from Guatemala when we got together for pizza. Since I had always been attracted to women who like to travel it was not long before we formed a bond. We also enjoyed movies, plays, concerts and Scrabble.

Our first spring trip was to the Sivananda Yoga retreat on Paradise Island in the Bahamas. As a yoga teacher I had been there several times before. Molly didn't care for the strict regimentation of the retreat but we found it fairly easy to ignore. Our next trip during the summer was a wonderful visit to Paris with all its great museums and unique restaurants. From there we flew to Italy, explored the Amalfi Coast and the remnants of the Pompeii Volcano eruption. We also drove to Rome and found it very easy to get around. We talked about traveling together next year to Israel.

I looked forward again to returning to teaching at Lincoln H.S. in the fall. I received an evaluation from my Assistant Principal, Mrs. Raybum, which was generous in all categories. I became friendly with her and we met for a chat every month or so.

I did not win a Presidential Award but certainly had not expected to do so considering all the time I lost teaching when I could not get a full time job and had numerous bipolar episodes. But Mrs. Stillman and I developed a cordial relationship and had many discussions regarding improving education in general and at Lincoln H.S. in particular. Mrs. Stillman was very bright, ambitious and hard working. She entered a Ph.D. program at Northwestern University that required 40 miles of commuting each way through downtown traffic three days a week.

Bryce Canyon National Park, Utah

I had been commuting between Rodgers Park in the northern most section of Chicago and Harvey, Illinois in the southern suburbs. Although I had two pleasant teachers riding with me during rush hour and snow storms it led me to look for a condo in Homewood, a small town five miles from Lincoln H.S. with a good library and well equipped fitness club. There were several parks nearby and a colorful bike path. By the time school started in Fall I moved from the north side of Chicago to the south side. It was like moving to a small town from a large sophisticated city.

In a few months I discovered the Homewood Izaak Walton Preserve, a small private park independently managed with three ponds, a prairie and a hilly wooded area. It had an interesting group of trails that I found satisfying for running after school. The ambiance of the preserve reminded me of the writings of H. D. Thoreau in his classic book "Walden". After several years I had taken thousands of photographs of the Preserve in all seasons at all times from before sunrise to after sunset. Since I lived just across the street from the Preserve I could very easily take my tripod to a suitable spot in the Preserve in several minutes. I reread "Walden" and found many passages that closely described the slides I had taken. With the help of the Lincoln H.S. AV department I coordinated the best photos with the appropriate passages in "Walden". We then used music from the Vivaldi's "Four Seasons" to provide a background for the slides.

When the project was complete I arranged to present it to the local Sierra Club, the Audobon Club, Social Clubs, Nature Clubs and school programs. I then hired a video company to transfer the slide program to video tape and made a number of copies of the video tape which was presented on local cable stations. I submitted a copy of my "Walden" tape to Chicago's public TV station. Although they were impressed with the program as a "labor of love" they could not use it because their budget for a half hour nature program was $500,000 and my program was made for $2,000.

During this time I also produced slide programs on "Kirlian photography" and "Is it art or is it Science?" which found an audience in many art and science clubs in the Chicago area. Photography became a passion for me and I arranged for many one-man exhibits of my work at local galleries. I also won a first place award in the annual Sierra Magazine photo contest and a first place in the annual Kodak "Best Picture of Chicago Contest"—an all expense paid one week trip to Hawaii for two. Molly and I arranged a fantastic trip to Maui and Kuai.

After returning from Italy with Molly, my friend from the Science department, Robert, and I set out on a camping trip driving through the American Southwest stopping at National Parks and scenic areas along the way—Arches National Park, North and South Canyonlands, Bryce Canyon National Park, the Grand Canyon National Park (North and South rim), Capital Reef National Park, Zion National Park, Great Sand Dunes National Park, Mesa Verde National Park, Silverton and Urey, and Rocky Mountain National Park. The trip was a fantastic opportunity to further develop my photography skills that were used to build up a collection of travelogues which I presented to assisted living homes as well as other groups.

As we began the trip I had a mild feeling of anxiety that I might develop depressive symptoms similar to those I had fifteen years prior when I drove out to Yellowstone National Park with several friends. To combat my worries I tried to remain as active as possible. Whenever Robert suggested resting after a hike to enjoy the scenery I urged him to go on before stopping for dinner. After dinner I suggested we walk off our dinner before setting up camp for the evening. Near the end of our trip I took a raft trip down the Arkansas River while Robert stayed in camp and did his laundry. Robert was quiet healthy, about my age and an ex football player. About half way into the four week trip I lost practically all my anxiety and felt naturally very energetic. I called Molly several times during the trip to tell her how great all the parks were and that I would like to take a similar trip with her in a few years. It's hard to say which the "best" park was. They each had a distinctive character of their own. Although our tent was big enough for two people, the weather was dry and I enjoyed sleeping out under the stars.

Zion National Park, Utah

When I returned to Chicago Molly and I prepared for a one month trip to Israel. Mary had a married daughter who lived in Kibbutz Nahshon—half way between Tel Aviv and Jerusalem. Her daughter arranged for us to stay and work on the Kibbutz. My job was mainly maintenance of the irrigation system used in the field where we grew Almond trees, but also included work in the garden, the kitchen and a small factory that exported plastic bags of various sizes. The factory was the most profitable of all endeavors in the Kibbutz.

We also took a week off to drive around the country and visit the colorful, historical towns. Most exciting was a tour we took into the scenic Sinai Dessert, Egyptian Territory where we slept at the base of Mount Sinai and awoke at 2:30am to climb historic Mount Sinai, planning to reach the summit at sunrise. We climbed during a full moon for an eerie experience. The view was unusual and spectacular, but more surprising was about ten individual religious groups of different denominations that also had climbed to the top. Each group was singing prayers in their own language. After a while we began the steep decent to the Monastery of St. Catherine—maintained by an order of monks for 1,500 years. I wandered off by myself and found a room partially filled with skeletons of skulls. I heard each skull at one time belonged to one of the high priests of the Monastery. The climb was one of the most spiritual experiences I've had.

We also toured Haifa, Tsvat, the Golan Heights and Tiberius on the Galilean Sea. The most fascinating "town" was the underground old city of Jerusalem. Some of the rooms of homes 2,000 years old were reconstructed with inlay tile floors and assorted pieces of wood furniture that looked band new. Our walk up the Via Dolorosa was crowded and filled with shops selling mostly a wide variety of clothing.

Grand Canyon National Park, Arizona—Sunrise

After our travels were temporarily finished I settled in Homewood and made arrangements with Molly to go up to Evanston and stay with her for the weekend three times out of a month and she would come down to Homewood and stay with me once a month. There were plenty of activities in the north suburbs of Chicago and there was a laid back, low key feeling to the south suburbs of Chicago. The south suburbs had quite a few dance halls, probably Willowbrook being the best known. I went dancing twice a week and found a woman who I began dating once a week. Pat had a great sense of humor and was sexually alluring. Molly came down for Valentine's Day weekend prepared for a sensual as well as sexy experience. She arrived about 2 o'clock and came up to my desk while I was finishing some school work. She noticed a very sexy Valentine's Day card from Pat sitting on my desk and gathered up her belongings and went out to her car. I followed behind her trying to "explain" about the card which was really unexplainable. She drove back to Evanston and I felt really horrible inside with a terrible sense of loss. It's hard to put into words the emptiness I felt, how difficult it was to teach my classes with images of Molly passing through my mind.

I sent her a bouquet of flowers and tried to get her to talk to me but she kept her distance. I forgot the details but we arranged to meet together with a female psychologist and each of us would tell the story of how we felt about the weekend and listen to the psychologist's opinion of the situation. Molly began by telling how hurt she was that I did not keep my promise of fidelity I replied that I did not recall offering any promise of fidelity, that I had very strong feelings for her but when the occasion came up I felt free to get involved with another woman. The psychologist suggested that we continue our relationship based on the fact that I was honest with Molly and it is very difficult to find men today who are honest with their girlfriends.

Molly and I continued our relationship and I felt much relieved. We planned our next summer trip to the Pacific Northwest that included visits to Crater Lake N. P., The Columbia River Gorge area, Mount St. Helens' National Park, Mount Ranier National Park, Olympic National Park, Victoria British Columbia, Bouchard Gardens, Banff National Park and Lake Louise. We combined camping with staying at park lodges. It was a wonderful trip and we looked forward to many more.

Capitol Building—Victoria British Columbia

I worked diligently on my photography putting together travelogues on each of the trips we took and arranging to present travelogues for assisted living homes, schools and social groups.

Politics took center stage at Lincoln H.S. when I returned from my wonderful summer travels. After a number of moderately successful years our principal decided to pursue his interest as a pastor for his "flock" and resigned. One of the Assistant Principals who served the school well was overlooked for the position as Principal most likely because he was white in a school where the student body was about 95% black. After a thorough interviewing process Mr. Hicks was hired as the new Lincoln H.S. Principal. He had a good reputation as football coach for a Junior High school in down state Illinois for nearly twenty years and had taught social studies for one year. His secretary had to correct the English in his correspondence. Any talk amongst the teachers regarding the hiring of our new principal was done behind closed doors.

In the meantime a faculty meeting was called by Mrs. Stillman to decide what direction our school should go at this time. I had been teaching about six or seven years at this point compared to the average teacher who had taught over 20 years. I had been warned by several teacher friends that the rule to follow at Lincoln H.S. was "keep your mouths shut and collect your paycheck" I thought I had a sensible idea and the right to express it so I recommended that we identify the basic problem areas of the school and then set about finding ways to correct them. My suggestion was overlooked and Mrs. Stillman brought up the fact that our school mission statement hadn't been revised in the last five years. She brought up the point that our mission statement needed revision and that a group of forty volunteers, faculty, students, board members and administrators should meet on a regular basis over the next six months for the purpose of bringing the one paragraph mission statement up to date. The faculty seemed to find much merit in Mrs. Stillman's recommendation and left the meeting with a feeling of much exultation. I remained seated until everyone left the room while a feeling of great sadness overcame me.

The following day I was sitting at lunch with a few of my fellow teachers "Well, she is at it again." Betty said. "We need a new mission statement like we need a new hole in our heads. What is this all about?" Carol asked. Most everyone knew Mrs. Stillman was in the process of getting a Ph.D. in education at Northwestern University. After most school hours she commuted from Lincoln H.S. to Northwestern, a distance of forty miles through downtown traffic. Planning and carrying out a project such as modifying a mission statement could be used to help meet her requirements for the Ph.D.. A suggestion was made amongst our lunch group to form a petition saying that we don't want to waste a half year of our time rewording a mission statement that has been adequate for the last five years. Sue and Jane volunteered to write the simple petition and I volunteered to make the rounds of faculty before classes started in the morning. I began early and collected more than fifty percent of faculty signatures in just two days. The only person who refused to sign the petition had ambitions of becoming an assistant principal and wanted to demonstrate she was a team player.

On the morning of the third day I came in later since I had more signatures than were needed. When I opened the door to my classroom I saw Mrs. Stillman standing near my desk. I don't believe I ever saw any administrator as angry as she was. Her face was nearly beat red and she was breathing deeply as she inquired "How dare you? How dare you attempt to ruin our work on a new mission statement?" I remained very calm and quietly said that I would stop collecting signatures. Of course my good relationship with Mrs. Stillman was destroyed. Did I do the right thing? If I acted simply in my best interests the answer would have to be no. But if teachers continue to live in fear of using their freedom of speech I believe there is no hope for truly improving education in our schools.

I have completely forgotten how I found myself as a member of the "Climate Committee" a group of administrators including assistant principals, deans, counselors, department chair persons and of course the principal. The purpose of this newly formed committee was to give each person a chance to express their ideas as to how the atmosphere in the school could be improved. As the time for the next meeting of the committee approached I spoke with several of the committee members. Trudy Beckmann told me that she had heard of several cases where teachers appropriately reprimanded students and the students went to Mr. Hicks complaining that he/she was being treated unfairly by the teacher. Mr. Hicks called the teacher to his office and made it clear that he wanted all students treated with respect in Lincoln H.S. I was also reminded by a group of teachers that the underlying motto of Lincoln H.S. was "Keep your mouth shut and collect your paycheck". Our paycheck was substantial and most teachers had children to put through college. I was told a sad story of a very good social studies teacher years ago who spoke up in the presence of the principal and later found that his teaching assignment was changed to five study halls a day.

I spoke with several teachers about speaking out at the next climate committee meeting. I also spoke to the president of the Teachers Union. He said I had a right to speak up and that he would sit between me and the principal. The night before the meeting I couldn't sleep. Under such circumstances I often left my condo and ran around an open field nearby rehearsing what I would say in the meeting the next day. During the committee meeting my turn to speak came near the end of the meeting. A few teachers had spoken critically of Mr. Hicks methods but they had twenty five years or more of experience at Lincoln H.S. and knew that their positions were not in jeopardy. Not many committee members paid attention to them. I spoke in a loud firm voice recalling that when I was in high school students lived in fear of being sent to the principal's office for misdemeanors. The Principal inevitably supported his teachers. Mr. Hicks was a large man. When he would get angry his face would blow up and turn red as possible for a black man. My words were short and to the point and the next thing I remember I was having a beer at the local tavern with the Teacher's Union President. I asked him if he felt I was out of order in my comments. He said "No".

Several months later I went to the department office to get our schedules for the following year. In the meantime things were fairly quiet at Lincoln H.S. A questionnaire was made out consisting of about one hundred questions giving teachers at all three high schools in the district a chance to rate their principals on a large variety of duties, attitudes and skills. Mr. Hicks came in with the lowest overall score.

In the meantime I questioned probably the best student I had in honors physics about the progress of the "Mission Statement Committee". She had been appointed to the committee months ago. She said she resigned from the committee some time ago, "They weren't doing anything".

When I first looked at my schedule for the following year I was literally in a state of shock—three classes of regular physical science and two classes of "essential physical science classes" (lower level, all sophomores). Our department chairperson was in the science office when I looked at my schedule and she could see my state of mind. In a cold manor she said "Saralyn Richard is my immediate supervisor and her boss is Mr. Hicks." She was making it clear she was not responsible the change in my schedule. At the end of the day I went to Saralyn and asked her if there was anything she could do to help me get my old schedule back. She replied, "He (referring to Mr. Hicks) could punish me worse than he has punished you." I was highly agitated, left the school and went to a local gas station to get some gas. I pulled out into the street without looking in all directions and was hit on the right side of my car by another car. The accident was clearly my fault and I don't remember the details of getting the cars fixed.

I was able to see my doctor in the next few days. She could tell very clearly that I was not in a position to teach my classes and told me to take ninety days off from my regular routine and use the time for vacations. I began by flying to Florida, visiting my mother and relaxing. Then I flew to Nassua and spent a week at the Yoga Retreat on Paradise Island. Talking with some of the guests at the retreat helped to focus on the present. I usually found that people who practice Yoga are very interesting.

Death Valley—Rocky Floor

Death Valley—Sand Dunes

When I returned to my mother's condo I planned the next part of my vacation. I was in the habit of traveling with friends but this time I went alone. First flying to LA and then driving to Death Valley. It was April and the weather was perfect. The Valley floor stretched for more than fifty miles and I often felt I was on another planet. There were canyons, large boulders, sand dunes and the snow covered peaks of California mountains at a height of over 11,000 feet could clearly be seen from an elevation of several hundred feet below sea level.

After leaving Death Valley, I drove to Sequoia National Park and stayed in a cabin. The altitude of the park was much higher than I thought. There was much snow still on the ground but there was also much wood for use in the pot bellied stove. The giant trees seemed to reach up into the clouds and once again I seemed to be traveling on a foreign planet.

I expected Yosemite National Park to be quiet in April but I forgot it was California school vacation and hundreds of students were on field trips. Also the highlands were still snow covered and I was confined to the valley. But the valley was warm and most trees and bushes were in full bloom which made for many good photograph opportunities. The best shot I got was at night with a full moon on one side of the sky lighting up Yosemite Falls and comet Hale Bopp on the other side of the sky with its tail shining brightly. I submitted pictures of the scene to astronomy magazines. They sent thank you notes but no publications.

Upon returning to Lincoln H.S. I continued to teach my physics classes for the rest of the year and planned a driving trip through New England, Prince Edward Island and Nova Scotia with Molly. Driving the Cabbot Trail at the north end of Nova Scotia was the highlight of the trip for us along with Peggy's Cove. I can still see clearly in my mind the winding road that climbs high along the ocean. The White Mountains are my favorite area in New England and I climbed Mount Adams above tree line and into the clouds. I returned just as a thunderstorm struck. We also stopped in central Vermont to visit my uncle Harry on Sunset Lake and were treated to some freshly caught Trout dinners.

Once again when I returned to Lincoln H.S. I went first to my new classroom which was a slightly remodeled day care center with a storage area in the back. There was no equipment for experiments. The room was isolated from other science classrooms. Two of my friends from the science department came to visit and asked if there was anything they could do to help with my situation. The principal of Lincoln H.S. acted as a dictator. I didn't see anything that could be done. I went back to the storage area and cried for a while but then I began to see that my situation was much better than it was before coming to Lincoln H.S. I had a full time job, my salary was good and I had a satisfying life outside of teaching. It was possible to improve the classroom by ordering appropriate equipment for student's experiments. I looked up the Junior High school records of some of my new students and found they had an average reading level between third and fifth grade. Two new students (Hispanics) could not read English but were very well mannered and a delight to have in class.

One of the biggest problems my students had in learning was the lack of ability to concentrate on a subject for more than five to ten minutes. To help them in this area we had a drawing lesson once a week when students chose one of the posters I had put up and attempted to draw the subject. I found that practically all the students worked on their project for the entire class time. If they needed help I gave them some assistance to get them back on track. We also spent one day a week watching a National Geographic video and each student wrote a summary of the video which they got credit for.

In terms of behavior I had a range of students from very cooperative to belonging in a correctional institution. One student, Charles, never sat down during the first ten minutes of class. He spent his time annoying the girls and attempting to steal items from my desk. I checked with counselors and found that he had received more detention slips than any other student in his class. I gave him a detention slip three or four times a week. When I turned around with my back facing the class to write on the black board students would throw paper, pencils and pens at me.

As I got more discouraged I went to one of the deans to discuss my situation. I told him that the president of the faculty union had an encouraged me speak up and he felt that nothing I had said would put my former teaching position in peril.

A new Physics teacher, Peter, was hired to teach what had been my Physics classes. He didn't care for the assignment and was determined to go to a good law school to become a lawyer. I was paid to help him get acclimated to Lincoln H.S.

Here I was paid to answer questions from the new physics teacher who took my place as I struggled to keep order in my classes with 4th grade reading skills. The dean laughed heartily, "Don't you know the Faculty Union President sleeps with the Administration?"

Mr. Hick's next move was to get his Assistant Principal Mr. James to "observe" one of my classes. I had assigned the class to read and study one page of our book and be prepared for a quiz the next day when he came to observe. During the quiz I noticed one student with his book open copying the answers from the book. Mr. James said to him politely, "Please close your book." When a student raised his hand Mr. James yelled at me, "Mr. Saxon, answer this student's question." I remained calm on the outside but was furious on the inside. I continued to take abuse from Mr. James until the end of the class when I walked out. Again as I left the school I was shaking and very anxious.

When I returned to Lincoln H.S. once again I realized my days at the school were over. The advantages of a very good paycheck might not be worth the mental anguish of teaching in a cesspool of a school. I went on sick leave the following day on my doctor's direction and told Mr. Peters the schools personnel administrator that I needed more time to work through my situation.

Of all the relationships I had, the one with Molly meant the most to me. I drove up to Evanston and we took a walk. It had been close to 100 days since I had seen her and when she told me that during the time I was gone she met another man that she started dating. I wasn't entirely surprised. We did agree to remain friends and see each other regularly as well as continue taking summer trips together. I had started seeing Pat again and things were relatively simple.

I soon found out that Molly's new boyfriend was also seeing other women which began to upset her. She asked me if I would join her on a seven day cruise to Alaska and even though I had taken a 14 day trip ten years before with Paula I said yes. Except for the increased crowds in the Alaskan towns it was a wonderful trip especially the hikes into the hills above the towns.

Now that I had more free time I volunteered for work in the Izaak Walton Preserve which I liked very much. My main work was trimming branches that began to grow into the many trails in the Preserve. I was also involved in maintenance of trails. Of course I continued teaching Yoga at the health and fitness Club and at the Homewood Jewish Community Center. Photography remained my passion and I remained active in the Park Forest Camera club. I arranged for more one-man exhibits and gave travelogues throughout the south side.

Money remained an issue since I had worked fulltime only seventeen years. Although the details are very hazy I had quite a few meetings with a gentleman from the teacher retirement system who arranged a reasonable yearly disability settlement for me.

Rather suddenly I found myself entering a very unpleasant depression. I saw my psychiatrist in person and he recommended one of the newer anti-depressants. Since he planned on being gone for some time he left me the name of a colleague who would be available while he was gone. The feelings of hopelessness and helplessness, the loss of confidence in myself which had been gone for so long felt familiar. I didn't want to be alone yet felt alone when I was with other people. I said very little. With Molly's encouragement I went to a party and tried to pay attention to the people who were talking. I saw my psychiatrist's colleague once and continued on the anti-depressants. I was able to keep up my responsibilities and gradually the depressed mood lifted and I was myself again in less than two months. No hypo manic mood followed that I was aware of.

On the last day of the spring semester I went back into the school and to my physical science classroom. I was surprised to find that my desk which I had always kept in the front of the room was now in the back of the room. A small thin black woman was sitting at the desk. I went up to her and introduced myself as the teacher of the physical science classes she had just finished teaching. Her name was Lakesha. I asked why the desk was now in the back of the room. She explained that when she first started teaching these classes objects like paper, pencils and chalk were thrown at her whenever she turned her back to the class. From her current position in the classroom no objects were thrown.

She went on to say that before coming to Lincoln H.S. she had really wanted to be a teacher. Now that she had two and a half months experiencing teaching five lower level classes each day she knew that she never wanted to be a teacher. I asked if I could take a look at her record book. She said yes and pointed out the good attendance in her classes. She had given one test during the time she taught. The grades were poor. I told her I appreciated the effort she made and let her know that many of the classes I had taught were far more considerate and satisfying to teach. I wished her good luck and said goodbye. I left the school and never returned.

A week later we had a barbeque lunch in our condo complex and an elderly man I had never seen before came carrying his school yearbook. The yearbook was dated in the late 1940's from Lincoln H.S. It was edited beautifully. Lincoln H.S. was rated as the highest ranking high school on the south side of Chicago. What happened? I'm not going to answer that question. It would only arouse confrontation.

I kept in close touch with a good friend at Lincoln H.S. He informed me that the assistant Principal, Mr. James, who had harassed me, was fired the following year. He went on to say that the Principal, Mr. Hicks, was fired several years later for getting involved in affairs with women on the School Board and whatever changes were made in the school curriculum or scheduling led only to the deterioration of overall school performance. The state never intervened. I eventually lost contact with school affairs.

I had made up my mind. Although my academic career was certainly not as productive as it could have been, I saw no way to make it the dream I once imagined. My parents had settled in a retirement village in Florida and I was a frequent visitor on vacations. The opportunity for sports, clubs, dancing, shows, photography and new friends were more than I needed. In about a year I bought a condo and relocated to South Florida. I sought to enjoy the many aspects of retirement living.

Bipolar illness cannot be cured. I discussed my situation with my psychiatrist and he agreed to continue to offer care by phone every other month. So far this arrangement has worked out well. I have not had a bipolar episode during the twelve years since I have retired. Although I did have need for help with problems in daily living, dealing with the village administration and relationships with women, it has been said that everyone has problems and difficulties with day to day life, but it is how we handle these problems that make the difference. Men and women with bipolar illness have additional biochemical situations that can periodically erupt and lead to extreme moods that can make them feel incompetent, hopeless, fearful and unable to enjoy normal relationships. Or they may have abundant energy, enjoy sexual potency and have more competence than their peers. I've had horrible anxiety dreams where I am totally lost and can't find my way home, where I never completed my academic studies or even where my life was in danger. I've had dreams of making love with exotic women, finding large sums of money and of my parents returning to life. We all have fears and we all can experience ecstasy. Life is but a dream.

AFTERWARD

I had no family in Chicago and decided to retire to southern Florida where I had spent so many happy vacations. I had grown accustomed to the support of my psychiatrist and arranged to have a therapy phone conversation with him every two months. I continued with medication of 600mg of Lithium per day and 2mg of Klonopin per day. Although I had occasional mildly high and low moods I never had another depression or hypo manic episode.

Molly and I remain friends and went on cruise vacations to Norway, Australia and New Zealand and a River boat trip to Vietnam, Cambodia and the Mekong Delta, along with many other trips throughout the US.

I learned the importance of continuing to take Lithium and Klonopin during the cruise Molly and I took to New Zealand. I had forgotten to take sufficient medication for the trip and it was several days before we reached a New Zealand town to get to a pharmacy. I very suddenly became depressed for a few days. I sat and starred at the TV, would not eat in the dining room and had my dinner brought to my room. I learned that taking Lithium and Klonopin were essential for my mental stability.

Choosing to live in a retirement village was a good choice for me. There were many clubs to take part in, shows such as the Platters, Elvis Presley impersonators, dance performances and symphony orchestra concerts every week as well as dances, sing-a-longs, classes such as bridge, computer, art, stained glass, tennis and yoga.

I took a leadership role in a movie discussion group, an Astronomy club, Philosophy club and Yoga club. I devoted considerable energy in presenting photography and travelogue programs, not just in the village but also in the wider community. Ballroom dancing is very popular in southern Florida and I attended various dance groups twice a week. Dancing was my favorite activity as well as a wonderful way to meet women. Eventually I settled down to a relationship with a wonderful, loving woman who was kind and generous. We traveled to Sanibel Island in Southern Florida, the Grand Canyon National Park, Bryce Canyon National Park, Zion National Park, Capital Reef National Park and Monument Valley. We took a Caribbean cruise and a Mediterranean cruise from Barcelona to Istanbul, Athens and Venice.

Gaudi Architecture—Barcelona, Spain

Windmills on Mykonos—A Greek Island

Bow of Cargo ship in Mekong Delta, Vietnam

As my mother grew infirm I was able to help with shopping, driving and care of her condo. Eventually she developed Alzheimer's disease and needed fulltime care. My sister and I eventually brought her to assisted living in the home of a woman who satisfied all her needs and brought love into the remaining years of her life. It was very sad to see her gradually lose her faculties but just holding her tightly brought life into her frail body.

After about three or four years of retirement I developed recurrent headaches which limited the activities in which I could take part. I saw many doctors who claimed they had successful methods of treatment but they were all temporary at best. I maintained my leadership roles in clubs and my passion for photography—giving many presentations of my work and having one-man shows. I enjoyed singing in the village chorus and kept up a walking routine although I could not run. It continued being pleasant making new friends.

Citric acid crystals – photo microscopy